D0745691

# SPIDERS
# OF THE
# UNITED STATES

# SPIDERS
# OF THE
# UNITED
# STATES

## by

## Richard Headstrom

SOUTH BRUNSWICK
NEW YORK: A. S. BARNES AND COMPANY
LONDON: THOMAS YOSELOFF LTD

© 1973 by A. S. Barnes and Co., Inc.

A. S. Barnes and Co., Inc.
Cranbury, New Jersey 08512

Thomas Yoseloff Ltd
108 New Bond Street
London W1Y OQX, England

Library of Congress Cataloging in Publication Data

Headstrom, Birger Richard, 1902–
  Spiders of the United States.

  Bibliography: p.
  1. Spiders—United States.  I. Title.
QL 457.1.H4        595'.44'0973          74–37813
ISBN 0–498–07927–9

Printed in the United States of America

TO MY WIFE

# CONTENTS

# PREFACE

Those of us who like to get outdoors, especially to follow the byways of nature, often encounter spiders on our walks; indeed, those of us who stay at home often meet them too, for some species take up residence in our houses. And, of course, many of them are found in our gardens.

Spiders have long been held in ill repute, because of the venomous nature of some, and therefore are usually shunned at all times. Perhaps it is not quite correct to say that only some are venomous; actually all are, for that is how they kill their prey. But only a certain few large species that live in tropical countries are dangerous; with one or two exceptions all the species that most of us are apt to come upon are practically harmless. A bee, a wasp, a mosquito, the common house fly, even the neighbor's dog, are potentially more harmful than any spider and, what is more, are likely to attack us far more quickly than any spider, for spiders are naturally shy and retiring and are more disposed to retreat at our advance than to show any belligerence towards us.

Spiders are less generally known than other animals and yet these much maligned creatures deserve better treatment than we are inclined to give them. In appearance many of them rival animals of more distinction. In the diversity of their habits they can equal those of the insects or any other group of animals better known. In numbers they can hold their own as anyone will discover who might go and look for them.

For a long time I have felt the need for a small book that anyone might carry in a pocket while outdoors that would provide one with the identity of a spider whose name one might wish to know, within certain limits. For there are many spiders that only an expert or specialist can identify. On the other hand, there are many species that can immediately be recognized by some easily observed character or by a fairly distinctive color pattern. In general it is these that most of us are apt to come across and whose identity we would want to know.*

To keep costs down and have the book within a price range that would make it available to everyone, the tarantulas, trap-door spiders and their relatives, which are not true spiders and which occur chiefly in the South and West, as well as some families whose representatives are rarely encountered have been excluded.

That the present book might meet the objectives for which it has been designed and also be the means of introducing spiders to those of us who have hitherto ignored them but who might like to know more about them is the hope of the author.

* A pocket lens or magnifying glass will often be found useful in determining the identity of a spider.

# 1
# GENERAL INTRODUCTION

## THE DISTRIBUTION AND ABUNDANCE OF SPIDERS

Spiders are widely distributed throughout the world. They inhabit all land areas from the tropics to the polar regions, including arid deserts and mountainsides to the snow line. A few have even invaded the water. In short, they are found wherever they are able to find living food suitable to them.

The spiders represent a fairly large segment of the animal population. Some thirty thousand species have been described of which two thousand occur in the United States. You need only go outdoors and select any area, however small, and you would be surprised to find the number of spiders living there. It has been estimated that there could well be over 14,000 spiders in an acre of woodland and over 64,000 in an acre of meadow. The spider population of the United States easily amounts to an astronomical number.

## THE PLACE OF SPIDERS IN THE ANIMAL KINGDOM

In our present system of classifying animals the spiders belong to one of the primary divisions or phyla (sing. phylum) known as the

Arthropoda, a word which means "jointed foot" (Gr. *arthron,* joint; *pous,* foot). To this phylum belong such animals as the lobsters, crabs, shrimps, crayfish, water fleas, barnacles, insects, millipedes, centipedes, scorpions, mites, ticks, and spiders. The Arthropods comprise about 78 percent of all known animals and can be said to be the dominant group of animals on earth if the criterion of dominance is the number of species.

Each phylum of the animal kingdom is in turn divided into a number of subdivisions which are as follows: Class, Order, Family, Genus, and Species. Hence, if we were to classify a spider we would proceed in the following manner, using the common grass spider as an example:
Phylum Arthropoda
  Class Arachnoidea*
    Subclass Arachnida
      Order Araneae
        Family Agelenidae
          Genus *Agelenopsis*
            Species *naevia*
The scientific name of the common grass spider is then *Agelenopsis naevia.*

## THE FOSSIL RECORD

The spiders are ancient animals, for fossils from the coal measures of the Carboniferous Era show that they were in existence at that time. The ancestral stock from which the spiders came originated some time before this era, but there is considerable speculation as what this stock might have been. There is no evidence to show that spiders descended from any living or extinct groups of arachnids, nor for that matter that they evolved from any particular group of arthropods. It is very likely, however, that they may have been derived from the trilobites that lived in the Cambrian seas.

## SPIDER MYTHS AND FOLKLORE

There was at one time a maiden who had attained such skill in the arts of weaving and embroidery that the nymphs would leave

---

* The class Arachnoidea received its name from the Greek word *arachne* which means spider. The class includes, in addition to the spiders, the scorpions, harvestmen, mites, ticks and others but the name is appropriate because the spiders are the most abundant members.

the groves and fountains to go to gaze upon her work. She was Arachne, daughter of Idmon of Colophon in Lydia. Her work was so beautiful and of such excellent quality that many believed that Athene, the goddess of handicrafts and patron of the arts, had herself taught her. But Arachne denied having been the pupil of anyone, even of a goddess. So it came to pass that in her arrogance she had the temerity to challenge Athene to a test of skill. Athene was greatly displeased at the brashness of a mere mortal and attempted to dissuade Arachne from engaging in such a rash deed. But Arachne was adamant in her resolve and the two proceeded to the contest. Athene wove a tapestry showing the warfare of the gods and the fate of those that conspire against them. Arachne executed a tapestry depicting the love adventures of the gods and with such a high degree of perfection that Athene became enraged at the thought that a mere mortal should have developed such amazing skill and destroyed it with a blow from her shuttle. Whereupon Arachne, humiliated and shamed, proceeded to hang herself. At the sight of Arachne suspended by a rope, Athene took pity on her and willed her to live, but that the lesson should not be lost on her, the Goddess decreed that Arachne and all her descendants should continue to hang forever. The Goddess then changed the noose into a cobweb and the unfortunate maiden into a spider, condemned to perpetual spinning.

Throughout the ages, spiders have been regarded as evil creatures and in many legends they are pictured as villains and murderers. They have also been viewed as benevolent animals with magical powers and under certain conditions their sudden appearance as omens of good fortune. In many of the legends of the American Indians, the spider is often portrayed as a creature of considerable significance and importance and a potent force for good though the legends also acknowledge the animal as capable of trickery and duplicity. To the Decotahs the orb web is a symbol of the heavens from which come the power and mystery of the Great Spirit and in the myths of the Pueblos, the spider is assigned the main role in Creation. A legend of considerable antiquity is that of the Spider Woman of the American Southwest who is supposed to have invented weaving and of having been a teacher of the textile art to various Indian tribes.

To the spider have been attributed such virtues as industry, patience, and persistence: the legend of Robert Bruce who acquired new courage from watching the spider is well known. Equally well known is the rhyme of the Spider and the Fly which describes the duplicity of the spider, a theme that reoccurs in the Indian legends.

A number of curious beliefs are still current despite the rather sophisticated times in which we live. One such belief is that killing a spider will bring rain and another that the appearance of cobwebs on the grass in the morning foretells clear weather. The following couplet:

Spider in the morning is a warning,
Spider at night is a delight

speaks for itself. Although in some instances the appearance of a spider is considered to be unlucky, in others it is supposed to signify good luck and that the observer will shortly receive gifts, new clothes, money, or visitors. Black spiders are considered to be unlucky, and white ones lucky, but sometimes the colors are reversed and the spiders assume the opposite quality.

Many of the superstitions concerning spiders had their origin in a superstitious age and have been handed down from generation to generation without much attempt to examine their validity with the result that children are often supplied with a great deal of misinformation. Much the same can be said in regard to the popular prejudice toward spiders which is in part due to the general belief that the bite of a spider is dangerous and to a somewhat natural antipathy or aversion to "crawling things."— Neither, of course, is a valid reason to dislike these animals.


## THE CHARACTERISTICS OF SPIDERS

*What Is a Spider?*

Most of us know what a spider looks like and yet if we were asked to describe or define a spider few of us could do so other than to say that spiders are animals that spin silk. But many insects also spin silk.

As we have noted previously spiders belong to a division of the animal kingdom known as the Arthropoda. The arthropods are joint-footed animals, bilaterally symmetrical (that is, the chief organs are arranged in pairs on either side of an axis passing from the head, or anterior end, to the tail, or posterior end), and consist of a series of longitudinal segments. On all or on some of these segments there is a pair of appendages. All arthropods have an exoskeleton or supporting structure on the outside of the body containing a horny substance called chitin and which is flexible at intervals to provide movable joints. A lobster, an insect, and a spider have these characteristics in common but they also have differences which serve to distinguish them. Thus a spider can further be defined as an animal having its body divided into two principal regions, the cephalothorax and abdomen (the two united by a narrow waist), the cephalothorax bearing four pairs of legs, sessile eyes, and two pairs of jointed appendages, the chelicerae or jaws often provided with poison glands, and the pedipalps that are variously modified in the different families. Spiders are air-breathing animals, respiration being effected by structures called book lungs and tracheae or air tubes, and they are also provided with spinning organs of silk known as spinnerets. Spiders differ from all other arachnids in having unsegmented abdomens, in other words the abdomen is sac-like.*

The tarantulas, trap-door spiders, purse-web spiders and certain other closely allied forms are in a sense spiders but differ from the true spiders in several characteristics, the chief distinction being in the articulation of their chelicerae. In the tarantulas the chelicerae are paraxial, that is, they project forward horizontally and with the fang so articulated as to be movable in a plane more or less parallel to the median plane of the body. In the true spiders they are diaxial, that is, they project downward or, in some instances, obliquely downward and forward and with the fang so articulated as to be movable in a more or less transverse plane.

The tarantulas and their kin also have two pairs of book lungs whereas only one family of the true spiders has retained this four-lunged condition; furthermore in most tarantulas the coxa of the palpi also lacks the endite or maxilla which is used by the true spiders in crushing and cutting their prey.

The tarantulas and their relatives are essentially tropical and sub-tropical in their distribution, but many of them range into the temperate zones and some eighty or ninety species occur in the South and West. They are not included in this book, which is devoted exclusively to the true spiders that we encounter most frequently.

### The External Anatomy of a Spider

#### The Cephalothorax
A casual glance at a spider shows that its body is divided into two regions. These two regions are known as the cephalothorax and abdomen, and are connected by a narrow pedicel (Fig. 1). The cephalothorax, like the abdomen, is unsegmented but frequently the head and thorax, which have been fused together to form the cephalo-

---

* There is a single small family of spiders, Liphistiidae, in which the abdomen is segmented but representatives of this family have been found only in the East Indies.

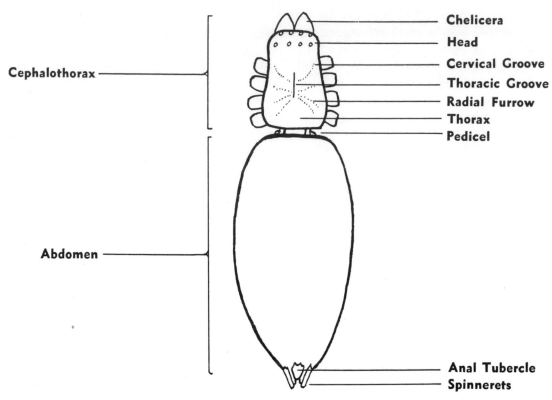

Fig. 1
Dorsal View of a Spider.

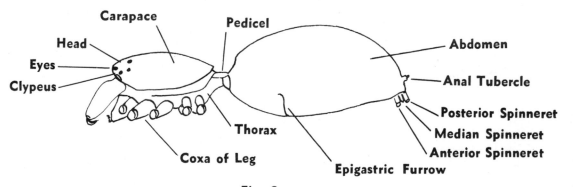

Fig. 2
Side View of Spider.

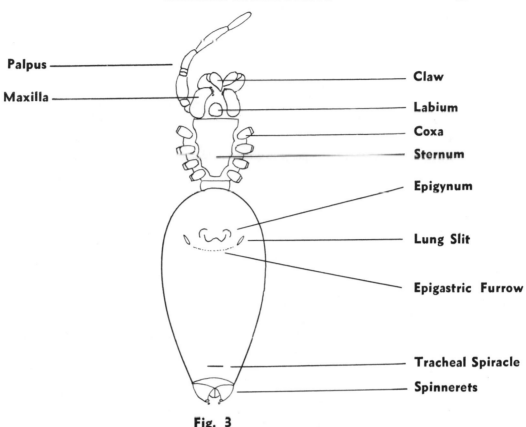

**Fig. 3**
**Ventral View of a Spider.**

thorax, are slightly separated by a furrow called the cervical groove (Fig. 1). The upper or dorsal surface of the cephalothorax is provided with a hard shield termed the carapace (Fig. 2), the lower or ventral surface with a hard plate termed the sternum (Fig. 3). Behind the cervical groove there is in many species a median depression called the dorsal, or thoracic, furrow or groove and radiating depressions that mark the internal attachments of the muscles of the stomach and of the legs (Fig. 1).

The cephalothorax bears the eyes, mouthparts, and legs and may vary considerably in shape and armature. In long spiders it is usually long and in short species may be wider than long. It is often surmounted with various spines, humps, and prominences of many kinds; in some species the eyes are situated on weirdly designed elevations. In the linyphiid spiders the carapace of certain males is grotesquely formed with deep pits into which the chelicerae of the females are fitted during copulation.

### The Head

The head is the part of the cephalothorax which bears the eyes and mouth-parts, the appendages used for seizing and chewing food. It may be slightly or not at all separated from the thorax but it is always easily distinguished (Fig. 1).

The head is divided into a number of areas to which special names have been applied. These areas are: the eye-space, the part of the head which is between the rows of eyes; the median ocular area, the space limited by the four median eyes and including that occupied by these eyes, also sometimes called the ocular quadrangle;* the ocular tubercle, the elevated part of the head on which the eyes are located in many species; the clypeus, the space between the eyes and the chelicerae; the face, the part of the head which is seen when the spider is looked at from directly in front and which includes the clypeus and a part or the whole of the eye-space; and the front, the anterior part of the head which is immediately in back of the clypeus (Fig. 4).

### The Eyes

The eyes of spiders are simple eyes, that is, they resemble the ocelli of insects and in none of them is the outer layer divided into facets. They are usually located near the front end of the head but in some cases they are grouped on a tubercle and in other instances they are so separated that they occupy nearly the whole width of the head.

Most spiders have eight eyes, which is the normal number, but some species have lost two or more of their eyes so that there are two-eyed, four-eyed, and six-eyed spiders. There is a tiny spider from Panama with only a single median eye and certain cave spiders are blind, having lost their eyes completely or at best retain only vestiges of them.

The eyes of spiders vary greatly in size; thus some of the hunting spiders have large eyes and keen vision, necessary to their way of life. Most spiders, however, are short-sighted and rely mostly on the sense of touch which has been sharpened at the expense of vision.

Two types of eyes are recognized: nocturnal and diurnal. Nocturnal eyes are pearly white in color and occur in spiders that live in the dark or frequent shady places. Diurnal eyes do not have the

---

* In the jumping spiders the term refers to the space occupied by all the eyes; in the wolf spiders the space occupied by the four posterior eyes.

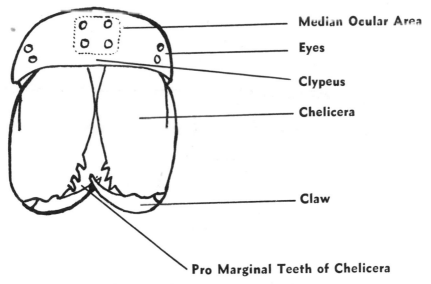

Median Ocular Area

Eyes

Clypeus

Chelicera

Claw

Pro Marginal Teeth of Chelicera

**Fig. 4**
**Front of Head of a Spider.**

pearly luster and are variously colored. The eyes of spiders may be either all of the same dark or light color, when they are said to be homogenous, or they may not all be of the same color when they are said to be heterogenous. The anterior medians are nearly always dark and circular; the others may be circular, oval, or triangular and either light or dark. In many spiders the eyes are provided with a tapetum which causes the eyes to shine in the dark when struck by light and which increases night vision.

The number and arrangement of the eyes on the head vary considerably and furnish characters much used in classifying spiders. The normal arrangement is two transverse rows of four eyes each. Certain terms have been given to the eyes, the terms being suggested by the relative position when thus arranged. These terms are the anterior median, the two intermediate eyes of the first row; the posterior median, the two intermediate eyes of the second row; the anterior lateral, the eyes at the end of the first row; and the posterior lateral, the eyes at the end of the second row (Fig. 5).

Sometimes the rows of eyes are curved and not in a straight line. When the lateral eyes of a row are farther forward than the median eyes, the row is said to be procurved; when the lateral eyes are farther back than the median eyes, the row is recurved. Sometimes the curvature is so great that the posterior median eyes are widely

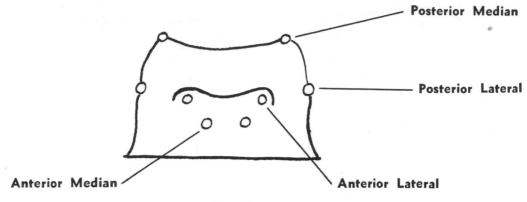

**Fig. 5**
**Eyes of a Spider.**

separated, when the eyes are said to be in three rows (Fig. 6), and at other times the eyes are in four rows, each pair of median eyes and each pair of lateral eyes constituting a row (Fig. 7).

### The Mouth

The mouth is situated between the base of the pedipalps and is suitable only for the reception of liquid food.

### The Chelicerae

The first pair of appendages of the head is the chelicerae or jaws which are the offensive weapons of the spider. They are situated in front of and above the mouth, from which they are separated by the rostrum or upper lip, and extend below and in front of the clypeus. Each chelicera consists of two segments, a large basal one and a distal claw-like one, the fang or claw (Fig. 4). In many spiders there is at the base of each chelicera, on the lateral face, a smooth, shining prominence called the lateral condyle and since it is absent in many families its presence or absence is a useful character in classification (Fig. 7A).

There is usually a furrow or groove in the basal segment of the chelicera for the reception of the fang or claw when not in use and there is also quite often a row of teeth on one or both sides of the furrow which are also of taxonomic importance (Fig. 4). Sometimes there is a brush of hairs, called the scopula, on the upper side of the furrow (Fig. 8).

The claw or fang, which is movable, is very hard, curved, and

**Fig. 6**
**Lycosa. Face Showing Arrangement of Eyes.**

**Fig. 7**
**Lyssommanes Viridis. Top of Head Showing Arrangement of Eyes.**

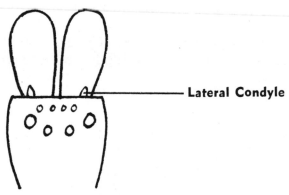

———— Lateral Condyle

**Fig. 7A**
**Head and Chelicerae of a Spider.**

pointed and is the part that is thrust into the prey. There are usually two delicate keels on the concave side of which the lower is invariably finely and regularly toothed, and on the convex side near the end there is a tiny opening through which the venom flows (Fig. 9). The position of this opening is such that it is not closed when the fang is inserted into a victim, thus permitting the poison to flow freely into the wound made by the claw.

The poison glands associated with the chelicerae are sometimes

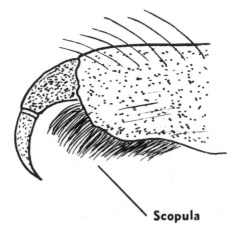

**Fig. 8**
**Chelicera of Agelena naevia Showing Scopula.**

contained within the basal segment, but in most spiders they are located in the anterior part of the cephalothorax as more or less voluminous pouches. The product of the gland is discharged through a long slender duct which opens near the tip of the claw (Fig. 10).

In some groups of spiders each chelicera is provided on its external face with a file-like series of ridges against which the inner surface of the femur of the pedipalp is rubbed to produce a sound. This is the stridulating organ.

### The Pedipalps

The second of the two pairs of appendages of the head is the pedipalps. They are situated one on each side of the mouth and are more or less leg-like in form, especially in the females, though they differ from the legs in the absence of a metatarsus. Each pedipalp consist of a series of six segments which are named beginning with the one next to the body as follows: coxa, trochanter, femur, patella,

Opening of Poison Duct

**Fig. 9**
**Tip of Claw or Chelicera.**

tibia, and tarsus (Fig. 11). The coxa bears a plate, called the endite or maxilla, which is the crushing part of the palps (Fig. 11). In many cases the internal border of the maxilla bears a brush of hairs, termed the scopula, and usually near its distal end a keel which is finely toothed and called the serrula which is of value in lacerating the prey and thus setting free the juices on which the spider feeds (Fig. 11). Between the two maxillae is the labium or lower lip which is the ventral wall of the head and more or less movable but in some cases it is fused to the sternum and is then immobile.

The coxa and the maxillae taken together form the trunk of the pedipalp, the remaining segments the palp. In the female the palpal tarsus is a simple structure and may or may not be provided with a single claw. In the male, where it is used as a copulatory organ, it is more or less enlarged and very complicated in structure. As the details vary in the different groups, much use is made of it in classification.

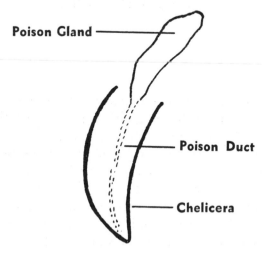

Poison Gland

Poison Duct

Chelicera

**Fig. 10**
**Poison Gland and Poison Duct of a Spider.**

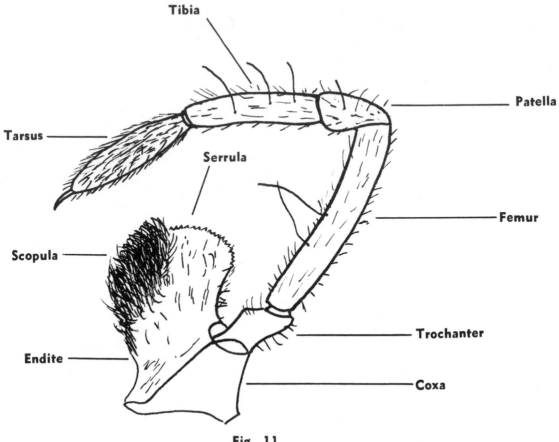

**Fig. 11**
**Pedipalp of a Spider.**

### The Thorax

The thorax is the part of the cephalothorax which bears the four pairs of legs. The plate forming the upper or dorsal surface of the thorax is called the tergum or carapace (Fig. 2). It extends forward on each side of the wedge-shaped hind end of the head and more or less covers the sides of the thorax. A median furrow or groove and several radial furrows that mark the point of attachment of muscles to the inner surface of the body wall are often present (Fig. 1). The plate forming the lower or ventral surface of the thorax and frequently heart-shaped in outline is called the sternum (Fig. 3). It occupies the entire space between the two rows of legs and on each lateral margin there are usually four notches for the reception of the legs.

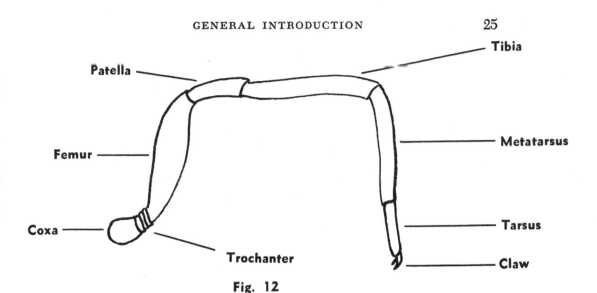

**Fig. 12
Leg of a Spider.**

*The Legs*

The legs are always eight in number. Each leg consists of seven segments; these are termed as follows, beginning with the one next to the body: coxa, trochanter, femur, patella, tibia, metatarsus, and tarsus which usually bears at its tip two or three claws (Fig. 12). The surface of the leg nearest the anterior end of the spider's body is called the prolateral surface, that nearest the posterior the retrolateral. In

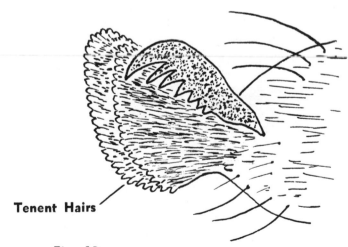

**Tenent Hairs**

**Fig. 13
Tip of Tarsus with Terminal Tenent Hairs.**

**Fig. 14**
**Metatarsus of Dictyna Showing Calamistrum.**

some spiders, as the crab spiders, the anterior legs may be turned so that the morphologically prolateral surface becomes dorsal, such a leg being called laterigrade.

In many spiders the tarsi are furnished with hairs that are dilated at the end and which are called tenent hairs (Fig. 13). When they occur at the tip of the tarsus they are known as terminal tenent hairs. They are also often found on the lower surface of the tarsus and metatarsus where they form a brush called a scopula. The hairs are of value in helping the spider to cling to smooth surfaces. The spiders that have the peculiar spinning organ known as the cribellum have on the upper margin of the metatarsus of the hind legs one or two rows of curved spines (Fig. 14). These spines constitute the calamistrum which is used in forming the hackled band characteristic of the webs of these spiders.

All spiders have at least two claws but in some species an unpaired median ventral claw is present which is quite small and sometimes difficult to see because of the bristles that often hide it, and which

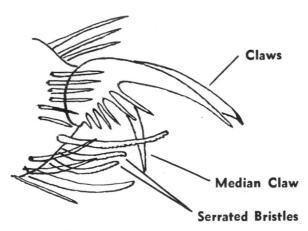

Claws

Median Claw

Serrated Bristles

**Fig. 15**
**Claws and Accessory Claws of a Spider.**

are frequently serrated when they are considered spurious or accessory claws (Fig. 15).

The legs of spiders vary considerably in length, in some species being long fine stilts. With so many legs it would seem as if the spider would experience some difficulty in synchronizing all of them when walking, which, of course, is not the case. When taking a step the spider moves the first and third legs of one side together with the second and fourth legs of the other side, the remaining legs going into action when these are at rest.

Not only are the legs often covered with hairs and spines but other parts of the body are also usually covered with these structures. Some of these hairs and spines lie flat against the integument and serve as a blanket; others, heavier or longer or more erect, serve the spider in various ways, as in spinning silk, preening, and capturing prey, and being extremely sensitive to touch or as receptors for chemical stimuli enable the spider to learn something of its surroundings.

### The Abdomen

The abdomen of the spider (Fig. 1) is more or less sac-like and quite variable in size and form. It is generally elliptical or oval but may be elongate, globose or angular. Because of the almost total lack of segmentation few distinct parts can be observed. In all spiders the abdomen is joined to the thorax by a slender stalk, the pedicel, which is usually concealed from view by the overhanging abdomen but in certain species which are ant-like in form it is quite conspicuous. Through the tiny channel of the pedicel pass the ventral nerve cord, a large artery, part of the alimentary canal, and frequently many small tracheal tubes, all necessary to the life of the spider.

The upper surface of the abdomen often shows a number of small rounded depressions which mark the internal attachments of muscles and in many species there is also an area leaf-like in outline and with scalloped edges called the folium (Fig. 16), which is sometimes covered with spots. The abdomen is often brightly painted and variegated with contrasting colors and in some spiders the upper surface is covered in whole or in part with a hard plate while in others it is armed with curious spines and processes which perhaps discourage attack by a predator.

On the lower or ventral surface of the abdomen the basal part is usually more convex than the rest of the abdomen. This area is termed the epigastrium and is separated from the more caudal part by a furrow called the epigastric furrow (Fig. 2).

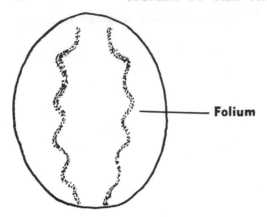

**Fig. 16**
**Abdomen Showing Folium.**

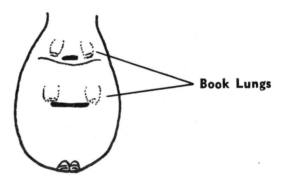

**Fig. 17**
**Abdomen of Hypochilus thorelli Showing Two Pairs of Book Lungs.**

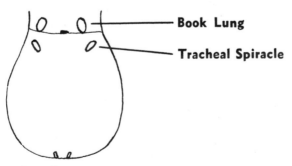

**Fig. 18**
**Abdomen of Filistata Showing Book Lungs and Tracheal Spiracles.**

On the lower or ventral surface of the abdomen are located the openings to the respiratory organs. These openings are of two kinds: one, the lung-slits, leads to the book lungs, lunglike saccular breathing organs that contain numerous thin folds of membrane arranged like the leaves of a book; the other, the tracheal spiracles, are the external openings of the tracheae or air tubes.

There may be one or two pairs of lung-slits. There is, however, always one pair except in one family of spiders and this pair is situated one at each end of the epigastric furrow (Fig. 3). The second pair, when present, is located behind the first pair (Fig. 17). All true spiders with the exception of one family have tracheae in addition to book-lungs and in most cases the tracheae have only one external opening or spiracle which is usually situated in front of the spinnerets but sometimes it is located in the middle of the ventral surface. In some spiders there is a pair of tracheal spiracles just behind the lung-slits and which can be distinguished from them by the external indications of the book-lungs (Fig. 18).

The internal reproductive organs open to the exterior through an opening called the genital opening which is located on the epigastric furrow between the lung-slits. Immediately in front of this opening, in the female, is a more or less complicated apparatus for storing the spermatozoa called the epigynum (Fig. 3). The epigynum varies greatly in form in different species.

At the posterior end of the ventral surface of the abdomen is the anus, the posterior opening of the alimentary canal, and which is situated on a more or less developed tubercle (Fig. 2). Below this anal opening are the spinnerets or spinning organs through which silk is emitted (Fig. 3).

### The Spinnerets

The spinnerets are finger-like in form (Fig. 2) and usually consist of three pairs, though in some instances there may be only two or even one pair. The pairs are designated as anterior, median, and posterior. The anterior spinnerets almost always consist of two segments each, the hind usually of two but sometimes three or even four, and the middle of none at all. The sides of the spinnerets are comparatively firm but the terminal part which constitutes the spinning field and which is always surrounded with hairs is membranous. Over the surface of the spinning field are distributed many small tubes through which silk is expelled and which are therefore called spinning tubes. Some spiders may have a hundred or more of these spinning

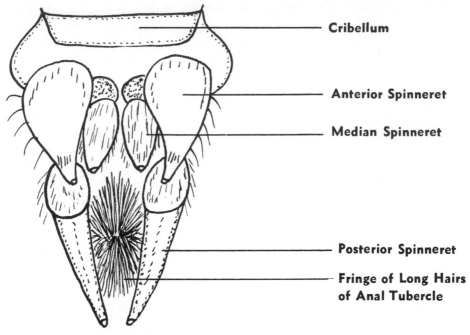

**Fig. 19**
**Posterior End of Abdomen of Oecobius.**

tubes on each spinneret but the number varies greatly in different species.

In certain families the spiders have an additional spinning organ which is located in front of the spinnerets and which is called the cribellum because of its sieve-like appearance (Fig. 19). The cribellum consists of a transverse plate which is usually divided by a delicate keel into two equal parts, and on which are numerous spinning tubes, the number greatly exceeding the number on the spinnerets but which varies in the different species.

## THE HABITATS OF SPIDERS

Spiders occupy a diversity of habitats. They may be found almost everywhere: in fields, meadows, and marshes, in or on ground, on trees and shrubs and herbaceous plants, on or near water, in practically every conceivable ecological kind of environment from underground caves to the tops of mountains.

They may be found on tall and low plants, beneath the dead leaves on the woodland floor and in the curled dried leaves of trees in winter, under bark, stones, and fallen logs, and inside and on the outside of buildings. Some species prefer dark and shady places where the humidity is high and live in caves, deserted mines, and cellars. Others that are water-loving live along the edge of ponds and streams and run over the surface of the water or dive beneath it and still others that are also water-loving occur on the shrubbery that overhangs the watercourses. Many spiders are found in tall grass, on bushes and trees where some of them run over the branches and trunk and hide beneath loose bark and in crevices while others hunt from leaf to leaf. And some of those that live on the ground dig burrows in which they spend part of their lives.

## THE HABITS OF SPIDERS

### The Food of Spiders

All spiders are carnivorous and subsist on the body juices of living animals that they subdue by means of their venom; only rarely can they be duped to accept dead food. Most of their prey consists of insects and, in this respect, the majority of spiders will take anything that comes along; but a few are selective and will refuse bees, wasps, and hornets and even beetles and bugs. Spiders may also feed on other spiders and a few species capture small fish such as minnows.

Spiders with weak jaws or chelicerae merely puncture the bodies of their victims and then alternately inject digestive fluid, which breaks down and predigests the tissues to a liquid condition, and suck up the liquified tissues by means of powerful muscles until only an empty shell is left. Spiders with stronger jaws crush the bodies of their victims to a pulp at the same time bathing it with quantities of digestive fluid. As the prey is rolled and crushed and the liquified tissues sucked into the mouth, it becomes smaller and smaller until finally only a small mass of indigestible matter remains.

Although spiders are extremely voracious and their appetite seemingly insatiable they are capable of enduring long periods of fasting. Many species can go weeks without water but some will not live if deprived of this necessary element for a few days.

**Fig. 20**
**Egg Sac of Miranda aurantia.**

**Fig. 21**
**Egg Sacs of Dictyna.**

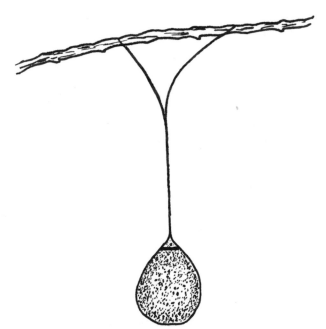

**Fig. 22**
**Egg Sac of Theridiosoma radiosa.**

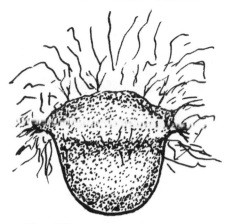

**Fig. 23**
**Egg Sac of Agelenopsis naevia.**

*How Spiders Capture Their Prey*

Spiders employ various means of securing their food. Some spiders, such as the wolf spiders and jumping spiders, run about in search of prey and pounce upon it whenever they can do so. Others, such as some of the crab spiders, hide in flowers and capture the insects that visit them. Still others spin webs or snares with which to trap the insects; these spiders usually wait on the web or on some vantage point nearby from which they can easily rush upon an entangled victim. Then there are the spiders of small size that live in the webs of the larger web-building species and feed on the smaller insects that are left untouched by the web spinners. Such spiders illustrate what is called commensalism, which means feeding at the same table.

*Eggs and Egg Sacs*

Spiders are oviparous, that is, they reproduce by laying eggs which hatch outside the body of the mother.

The life of a spider begins when a zygote or fertilized egg is formed by the union of a male sperm with a female ovum, which is believed to take place shortly after the eggs are laid. Just before the time of egg laying, the mother spider prepares a silken sheet on which the eggs are placed as they issue one by one from the genital opening and at which time they are covered with a syrupy fluid in which quantities of sperm have been discharged from the spermathecae where they had been stored prior to the time of egg laying. At this time the eggs have a very soft outer covering or chorion (shell) easily penetrated by the sperm. Once the eggs have been laid the female spider covers them with a silken sheet and molds the mass into the egg sac characteristic of the species.

Spider eggs are ordinarily spherical or broadly oval but their shape is frequently distorted by the weight of the mass of eggs within the egg sac. They may be white or colored pink, yellow or orange and in size they may vary from .4 mm. in the smallest spiders to several mm. in the largest. The number of eggs also varies according to the species. Some of the larger spiders may lay over 2000 eggs, whereas many tiny spiders may lay only one or two and perhaps no more than a dozen during their lifetime. Spiders of average size probably lay a hundred or so. Most spiders lay all their eggs at one time and enclose them in a single egg sac but others extend their egg laying over a period of time and enclose them in a number of egg sacs.

The egg sac is generally spherical (Fig. 20) or lenticular (Fig. 21) in outline but it may be pear-shaped (Fig. 22) or cup-shaped with a flat top (Fig. 23) or it may be of such a form as to remind us of a

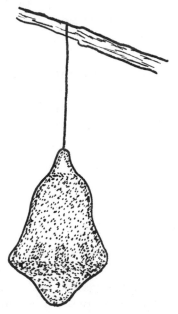

**Fig. 24**
**Egg Sac of Argyrodes trigonum.**

**Fig. 25**
**Egg Sac of Tetragnatha elongata.**

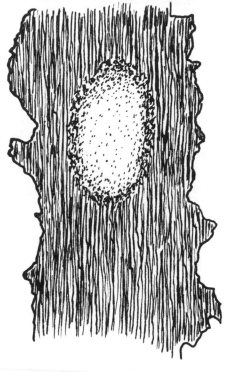

**Fig. 26**
**Egg Sac of Agelenopsis naevia.**

beautiful Grecian vase (Fig. 24). The egg sac is not a haphazard affair but usually a carefully made structure of a design characteristic of the species so that it is often as easy to identify a spider from its egg sac as from a study of the spider itself. The simplest type of egg sac is one that consists merely of a mesh of threads that hold the mass of eggs together and so delicate that the eggs can be seen through it. Another type consists of a fluffy mass of silk which effectively conceals the eggs but which has no definite form. Most eggs sacs, however, have a definite shape and are made of several layers of silk differing in texture. If the egg sac of the orange garden spider (Fig. 20), for example, is opened, it will be found that the eggs are enclosed in a silken cup which is surrounded by a thick layer of flossy silk and which in turn is enclosed within a firm, brown, closely woven outer covering.

In most egg sacs the outer covering is opaque but in some it is translucent. In some species the egg sacs look as if they had a covering of some kind of foreign material due to the presence of curiously twisted tufts of silk differing in color from that forming the rest of the egg sac (Fig. 25). In other species the spiders plaster the egg sac with mud, or add bits of wood, leaves, stones, and other debris (Fig. 26), presumably to make them less conspicuous.

The majority of spiders fasten their egg sacs in some relatively safe and secure place, as beneath loose bark. Others attach them to the side of a building, to the side of a stone, or to a twig or branch. Still others secure theirs to the side of a cliff in a damp situation that they frequent. Many spiders place their egg sacs in tall grass, on herbaceous plants, and on shrubs where they fasten them securely with a number of strong silken threads so that the storms of winter cannot tear them loose.

Since the survival of the species depends on the safety of the eggs it is not surprising that the egg sacs are fashioned with as much care and attention as the spider can command. However, eggs sacs that are placed in exposed situations are more elaborately made than those that are located in a burrow in the ground or surrounded by barriers of silken threads or those with which the mother remains until the eggs have hatched.

### Hatching and Development

Spider eggs usually hatch within a short time after they have been laid, in some spiders the egg shell being broken by a tooth on the base of the pedipalps. Depending on when the eggs are laid the young spiders may remain within the egg sac for a long time or they may emerge shortly afterwards. The young spiders or spiderlings that hatch from eggs laid in the fall in the North usually remain within the egg sac until the following spring.

As the outer covering or integument of all arthropods contains chitin it is necessarily hard and inelastic and cannot stretch to allow for the growth of the spider. Hence it must be shed periodically, a process called molting. But before the old integument or cuticula is shed a new one is formed beneath the old one; then the old integument bursts open and the spider, casting it off, emerges clothed in a soft integument which stretches to accommodate the increase in size. It soon hardens, however, and after a while it too must be shed to allow for further growth.

During the course of their development the young spiders increase in size but show no marked change in form. The most pronounced change occurs at the last molt when the sexual organs become completely developed. Previous to the last molt the tarsus of the pedipalp of the male is merely a club-like segment but when the cuticula is shed for the last time the exceedingly complicated sexual organ is revealed. In the females of such species that have an epigynum this organ is also not exposed until the last molt.

The number of molts a spider undergoes before it reaches maturity varies with different species. Small species molt only a few times, larger species a greater number. During the molt and until the new integument has hardened the spider is vulnerable to attack by animals that would not ordinarily attack it. Furthermore the mechanical difficulty of extracting its appendages from the old integument may sometimes result in the mutilation of these appendages and render the spider less able to survive in a hostile world.

## Autotomy and Regeneration

Like many other arthropods spiders are able to drop off an appendage and, in the case of young spiders, to regrow a new one but the replica does not attain the degree of perfection of the normal one.

This dropping off of an appendage, called autotomy, serves as a useful device from the viewpoint of protection and survival since a spider is often able to escape from the clutches of an enemy without greater loss than the losing of one or two appendages.

In its strictest sense autotomy, which means self-mutilation or the voluntary discarding of an appendage, does not occur among the spiders; a spider can discard an appendage only through visible effort, in other words, by exerting such force on a leg for instance that the tension on it snaps it off at its weakest point which is usually between the coxa and trochanter.

The loss of an appendage or two may not seriously inconvenience the spider but on the other hand it may have disastrous results. Thus the loss of the front legs of a crab spider, which are not only organs of touch but also offensive weapons, would greatly impair the spider's ability to capture prey. And mature males that have lost some of their front legs are at a distinct disadvantage when courting the females and may become easy victims to such females that are not cooperative.

*Courtship and Mating*

The spiders have gone to considerable lengths to make sure that they will continue to survive as a group. The union of the sex cells is accomplished in a most unusual manner and by means of specially developed organs. Instead of a primary intromittent organ the male has evolved a secondary one of wonderful complexity at the end of each of the pedipalps while the female in complement to the palpi of the male has developed an organ called the epigynum which is specialized to receive the male palpus, to store the sperms, and to transfer them to the fluid of the egg mass at the time of egg laying.

Prior to the actual mating, the actions of the male and female are fairly distinctive and are usually referred to as the courtship behavior. The first step on the part of the male, once he has become mature and capable of mating, is to transfer the sperms produced in the testes to the palpi, a process called sperm induction. This accomplished he must next find a mate.

As spiders respond to the conditions of their environment largely through the sense of touch it is to be expected that the male would rely mainly on the fine sensory hairs that cover his body and appendages to locate a female. Associated with the sense of touch is also an ability to distinguish various chemical substances; thus it is through this combined chemotactic sense that the male finds his mate by a scent that she leaves on the threads of her web or on any substratum on which she may have moved. Some spiders, such as the jumping spiders, have such keen eyesight that they can locate a female by sight alone; on the other hand some wolf spiders that have an equally keen vision depend on both sight and touch.

Locating a female is, however, only one step in the wooing of a mate. The female, conditioned to a predatory existence, would be more than likely to view an advancing male as suitable prey were she not made aware of his presence in some manner. Hence the male must announce himself in a way designed to let the female know that he is a prospective suitor. Consequently he initiates certain maneuvres, in which the female may later engage when she has reached a certain pitch of excitement, that are part of the courtship ritual and which, if all goes well, eventually lead to the actual mating.

In the web-building species these maneuvres consist essentially of the male signalling his presence by tweaking the threads of the female's snare and perhaps by moving his palpi and abdomen in a sort of dance. In the wandering spiders, especially in those species that have keen vision, the courtship ritual is more elaborate. Here the males often perform bizarre dances, wave their palpi or legs or both, display their ornaments if they have them, and strike peculiar attitudes. Whatever the extent of the male's courtship may be, if he is successful in lulling her normal instinct to view him as prey and in stimulating her to a point where sexual union is possible, she submits to his advances and mating takes place.

There appears to be a popular misconception that the female always kills the male after the mating act is over. This may be true in some species but in most spiders the sexes separate peaceably. Indeed, the male may even mate again with the same female or with some other female.

## Sexual Dimorphism

In many species of spiders the two sexes differ greatly in size, the males often being one fourth as large as the females and in certain species the males are real pygmies. In other species the males are about the same size as the females; however, in such cases the abdomen of the male is usually slimmer and is frequently covered with different kinds of hairs and patches of setae or the legs may be longer with a greater range of sensory perception, of value in evading the female. Some males have brushes of hairs or colored scales that are displayed during courtship and many have spines and spurs on their legs and chelicerae with which they hold the female during mating. In many species the males are more handsome than the females; in others the reverse is true, the females having beautifully painted and sculptured bodies. Finally, in some species the sexes are so markedly different in appearance that they were once regarded as two distinct species.

## Parental Care

In most cases when a female spider has laid her eggs and has enclosed them in an egg sac her duties as a parent are over. Some species, however, guard their eggs for a while and others help the spiderlings to emerge; the wolf spiders even carrying the young about on their backs until they are ready to fend for themselves, but as a rule spiders exercise little care over their offspring.

*The Longevity of Spiders*

Most of the spiders that occur in the United States live only about a year, though some species, like some of the wolf spiders, may live several years. Occasionally, others such as the large water spiders and the black widows may extend their life span to eighteen months, though normally it is only a year.

*The Winter Life of Spiders*

Spiders spend the winter in all stages of life, as eggs, young spiderlings of various ages, and adults. Species that spend this season of the year as eggs usually do so in egg sacs that are attached to plant stems, stones, and other objects, while those that overwinter as spiderlings and adults may be found beneath carpets of dead leaves on the forest floor and among the roots of mosses. Many adult spiders escape the rigors of winter in a special shelter such as a cave, a deep crevice, a burrow in the ground, or under the scales of bark or beneath stones.

*The Migration of Spiders*

We usually think of migration in terms of long distances, such as the flights of birds in the spring and fall, but actually migration is a movement of animals from one place to another, either regularly at certain seasons or irregularly in response to some special or unusual conditions of their environment and irrespective of the distance involved. Thus when a chill in the air presages the coming of winter spiders crawl lower on the trees where they have spent the summer or creep downward on the lower bushes and herbaceous plants where they have summered, tarry a while, and then continue to the ground cover of leaves and grass.

*The Venom of Spiders*

It is generally believed that all spiders should be feared and avoided because of the venomous nature of their bites but actually there is little reason for it. Most of our spiders are shy and timid and quite harmless and are unable to inject enough venom should they succeed in biting us to do us any harm. Some of the large wolf spiders will bite readily if handled carelessly and in people that are abnormally susceptible to arthropod venom may inflict a wound as painful as a bee's sting though the effects disappear much more quickly.

There are, however, several species that should be avoided at all times since they are generally considered dangerous. They are the several species of Latrodectus, known as the "widow spiders" and one species of Loxosceles known as the brown recluse spider. Anyone bitten by any of these spiders should obtain prompt medical attention.

## Methods of Protection and Defense

Although the chelicerae and poison glands are essentially offensive weapons they also provide the spiders with a certain measure of protection against their enemies. They are not the only means as spines and hairs serve the same purpose. Then many spiders elude the attention of a would-be predator by being colored like their surroundings or resembling some inanimate object as a piece of bird dung or a plant bud; some with elongated bodies and long legs look like pieces of straw and grass. A few even mimic other animals, especially ants, which are assumed to have few enemies. The ant-like spiders not only imitate the ants in body form but also in behavior, thus, for instance, moving about with their first pair of legs elevated like a pair of antennae.

## The Silk of Spiders

The silk of spiders is produced as a liquid by the silk glands and when drawn out of the spinnerets hardens on exposure to the air to form the familiar silken threads. The silken threads have considerable strength and elasticity, their tensile strength being said to be second only to fused quartz fibers and far greater than that of steel. The threads will stretch one fifth of their length before breaking. The finest threads are about a millionth of an inch in thickness and are invisible to the naked eye; most spider threads are not single fibers though they may appear to be.

Spiders spin different kinds of silk, which are used separately or in combination according to the purpose for which they are to be used. Spiders use their silk in many different ways: dragline; bridge line; trap line of the orb weavers; warning threads; ballooning threads; attachment disks; cells and retreats; hibernating chambers; molting threads; beds and chambers; egg sacs; nursery webs of the nursery-web weavers; sperm webs of the males; bridal veil of the crab spiders;

courtship and mating bowers of the black widow; barrier webs of the grass spiders and the aerial sheet weavers; sheet webs; orb webs, swathing bands; and there are others.

Of all the uses to which the silk is put, the dragline is doubtless the most important; it is the life line of the spider and is the one most commonly observed of all the silken threads. With the exception of a small group of primitive forms of the family Liphistiidae, it is spun by all spiders of all ages. Most spiders as they move about pay out the dragline behind them and which is fastened to the substratum at intervals by means of attachment disks. The jumping spiders jump from cliffs or the sides of buildings to escape a predator and float down gently on the silken threads of the dragline. Web spiders often drop from their webs on the dragline when threatened with danger and hide in the vegetation on the ground or remain suspended in mid air until all danger is past when they climb back up to their original position. The orb weavers also use the dragline as a trapline to detect the presence of an insect in the web and to outline the zones of their snares. The dragline is used, too, as a bridge by the spiders between two objects, as two trees or two herbaceous plants, or across a stream and it forms the supporting threads when they go ballooning. The tangled webs in our houses, often weighed with air debris and which we know so well as cobwebs, are mostly made of dragline silk.

## The Webs of Spiders

The webs of spiders, which are actually snares for trapping insects, vary greatly in structure though a few fairly distinct types can be recognized. The web of the domestic spider, *Theridion tepidariorum,* which is merely a maze of threads extending in all directions, illustrates the type of web which is usually referred to as an irregular net. In a sheet web the principal part of the web consists of a more or less closely woven sheet in a single plane and consisting of threads extending in all directions in that plane with no regard for any regular arrangement. A good example of a sheet web is that of the hammock spider, *Linyphia phrygiana.* A funnel web is similar to a sheet web but differs from it in having a tube extending from one edge and leading to a retreat. The common grass spider, *Agelenopsis naevia,* builds this kind of web.

The large conspicuous webs so often seen on vegetation during the summer are called orb webs. The characteristic feature of such a web is that the part contained within the supporting framework consists of a series of radiating lines of dry and inelastic silk on which has been spun a spiral thread of viscid and elastic silk. In some webs, such as that of the foliate spider, *Aranea frondosa*, the viscid thread extends in many spiral turns, such webs being called complete orbs; in others, such as that of the labyrinth spider, *Metepeira labyrinthea*, the viscid thread extends in few if any spiral turns it being looped back and forth on the radii, such webs being called incomplete orbs.

The web of *Hyptiotes* is distinctly triangular in outline and is known as a triangular web. Then there are the webs with hackled bands, such as those made by the cribellate spiders, and the composite webs that are composed of a sheet web and an irregular web, such as that of *Linyphia marginata*, and of an orb web and an irregular web, such as that of *Metepeira labyrinthea*.

In an orb web certain parts may be distinguished as follows: the bridge, which is the original thread spun by the spider between two objects on which it can move back and forth for the purpose of laying the foundation lines; the foundation lines, which are the silken threads that form the framework of the web; the radii, the radiating lines of the web; the hub, the center of the web; the notched zone, an area outside the hub in which there are a few turns of the spiral line; the viscid spiral, the circular turns that form the main part of the web; the free zone, an area untouched by the spiral line; the stabilimentum, a zigzag ribbon spun across the center or below the hub; and the trap-line, one or more threads that connect the retreat with the hub on

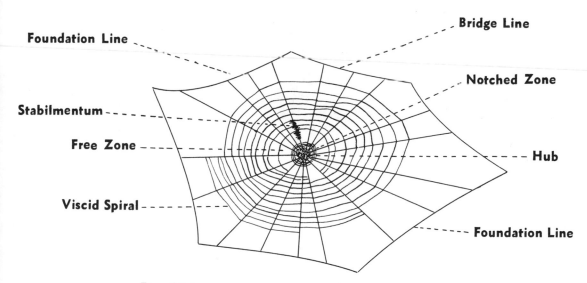

**Fig. 26A**
**Diagram of a Web of an Orb-weaving Spider.**

which the spider can pass back and forth and by means of which the spider can detect any disturbance on the web (Fig. 26A).

## The Ballooning of Spiders

Spiders usually move about from place to place by means of their legs but they also have another method at their disposal, sailing through the air.

When a spider feels the urge to go sailing through the air, it climbs to the top of some promontory, which may be the top of a spike of grass, or of some herbaceous plant, a stone or fence rail, in fact any elevated object, where it turns its face in the direction of the wind, extends its legs, and tilts its abdomen, and then spins out several threads of silk which are caught by the air currents and carried upwards (Fig 27). When enough threads have been spun to support the weight of the spider, it then lets go and is pulled into

**Fig. 27**
**Spider Preparing to Balloon.**

the air to be carried away on its silken parachute. It would appear that the spider would be at the mercy of the wind but it is able to exert some control over its "balloon" by pulling in and winding up the silken filaments or by spinning more of them.

It was once supposed that the aeronautic habit was the monopoly of a single species or limited to a certain time of the year but it is now known that it is not the exclusive right of a single species and that it can be indulged in at almost any time though ballooning most frequently occurs in the spring and fall when immense numbers of young spiders emerge from the egg sacs. At such times by their very numbers they attract our attention.

Small spiders may often be made to take off by blowing steadily against them and as it happens sometimes very tiny spiders, weighing an insignificant amount, are suddenly lifted into the air by air currents when they least expect it. Even the larger spiders when dropping on their draglines are frequently caught by the wind and blown some distance.

Most ballooning goes on at heights up to two hundred feet but sometimes powerful air currents carry the small aeronauts up as high as 10,000 feet. And that these ballooning spiders are often carried considerable distances is shown by the fact that they have been picked up by ships at sea several hundred miles from land.

In the fall of the year, spiders become greatly active and cover the fields and meadows with countless silken threads, many of which are spun by the spiders in unsuccessful attempts to fly and which remain suspended on the vegetation. These threads often form tangled sheets of silk that are sometimes picked up by the wind and deposited elsewhere, frequently far from their place of origin. This is the explanation for the showers of gossamer celebrated in prose and poetry.

## THE ECONOMIC IMPORTANCE OF SPIDERS

Since spiders occur in great numbers in any terrestrial community, it is fairly obvious that as predators they must play a significant role in the ecology of the habitat. It is said that they destroy annually a greater number of invertebrates than the highly regarded birds and if this is true their importance cannot be discounted.

Since the snares of many spiders are designed to catch flying insects, a high percentage of their catch doubtless consists of beneficial insects yet, on the other hand, the numbers of biting flies and annoying midges that their webs entrap show that they are of value in helping to control many destructive insects. Many of the hunting spiders, too, are known to concentrate on obnoxious species.

As agents of biological control they have been found effective in checking such destructive insect pests as the cotton worm, gypsy moth, pea aphid, and others. Their silken threads have been found useful in certain types of optical instruments and the Papuan natives employ their matted webs for lures and fishnets. And not only do they supply much needed fats and proteins to the diet of certain peoples but they also provide food for game fish and birds. Their unsightly dust-catching webs in our houses may be a nuisance but they render us a service in trapping flies and mosquitoes that have succeeded in getting through our window screens. Though a few of them are rather dangerous they so rarely come in contact with humans that their medical importance is negligible. In this regard none of them has been found to be a vector of any human disease and unlike their relatives, the mites, none is parasitic on man and his domestic animals. If spiders cannot be credited with being of value to man certainly they cannot be placed on the debit side of the ledger. In all likelihood their place in the scheme of things is a neutral one.

**Fig. 28**
**Dysdera crocata. Ventral Surface of Thorax Showing Cylindrical Coxae of First Two Pairs of Legs.**

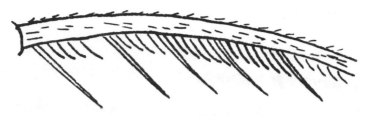

**Fig. 29**
**Mimetus interfector. Tarsus of First Pair of Legs Showing Spination.**

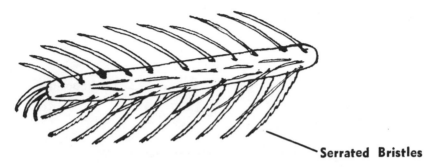

Serrated Bristles

**Fig. 30**
**Tarsus of Fourth Pair of Legs of Theridion Showing Comb of Serrated Bristles.**

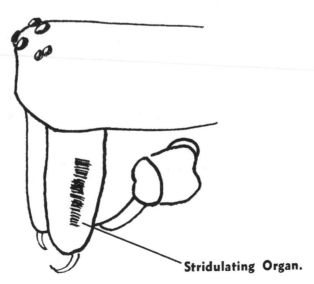

Stridulating Organ.

**Fig. 31**
**Chelicera of Lephthyphantes nebulosus Showing Stridulating Organ.**

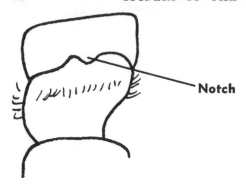

**Fig. 32**
**Trochanter of Leg Showing Notch.**

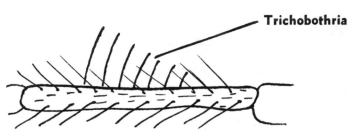

**Fig. 33**
**Tarsus Showing Trichobothria.**

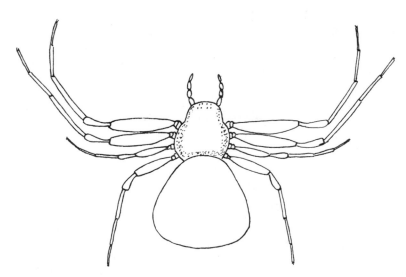

**Fig. 34**
**Misumena aleatorius. Showing Laterigrade Legs.**

# 2
# KEY TO FAMILIES

1a. Spiders With Two Pairs Of Book Lungs
(Fig. 17) ............................ Hypochilidae, 51
1b. Spiders With One Pair Of Book Lungs And
One Pair Of Tracheal Spiracles (Fig. 18).....
1c. Spiders With One Pair Of Book Lungs And
One Tracheal Spiracle (Fig. 3) ............
2a. With A Cribellum And A Calamistrum
(Fig. 14 and 19) ........................ Filistatidae, 63
2b. Without A Cribellum And A Calamistrum, . . . .
3a. Tarsi With Three Claws ................ Segestriidae, 66
3b. Tarsi With Two Claws ..................
4a. Coxae Of The First Two Pairs Of Legs
Long And Cylindrical (Fig. 28) ........... Dysderidae, 64
4b. Coxae Of All Pairs Of Legs Similar, Nearly
Globose .............................. Oonopidae, 67
5a. With A Cribellum And A Calamistrum ......
5b. Without A Cribellum And A Calamistrum ....
6a. Anal Tubercle Large And Fringed With
Long Hairs (Fig. 19) .................... Oecobiidae, 62
6b. Anal Tubercle Normal And Without A
Fringe Of Long Hairs ...................
7a. All The Eyes Dark In Color .............. Uloboridae, 52
7b. All The Eyes Light In Color ............. Amaurobiidae, 56
7c. Median Eyes Dark, The Others Light In
Color ................................. Dictynidae, 59

8a. Spiders With Three Tarsal Claws . . . . . . . . . .
8b. Spiders With Two Tarsal Claws . . . . . . . . . . . .
9a. With Six Eyes . . . . . . . . . . . . . . . . . . . . . . . .
9b. With Eight Eyes . . . . . . . . . . . . . . . . . . . . . . .
10a. Anterior Eyes In A Nearly Straight Row . . . . . Diguetidae, 69
10b. Anterior Eyes Not In A Straight Row . . . . . . . .
11a. With A Conspicuous Thoracic Furrow
     (Fig. 1) . . . . . . . . . . . . . . . . . . . . . . . . . . . Loxoscelidae, 71
11b. With An Inconspicuous Thoracic Furrow . . . . Scytodidae, 72
12a. Spinnerets In A Single Transverse Row . . . . . . Hahniidae, 194
12b. Tarsi Long And Flexible . . . . . . . . . . . . . . . . Pholcidae, 80
12c. Tibiae And Metatarsi Of First Two Pairs
     Of Legs With A Series Of Very Long Spines
     And A Series Of Shorter Spines Between
     Each Two Long Ones (Fig. 29) . . . . . . . . . . . Mimetidae, 151
12d. Tarsi Of Fourth Pair Of Legs Furnished
     With A Comb Consisting Of A Row Of
     Strong, Curved, And Toothed Setae (Fig. 30) . . Theridiidae, 83
12e. Tarsi Of Fourth Pair Of Legs With
     Spurious Claws . . . . . . . . . . . . . . . . . . . . . . . .
12f. Tarsi Of Fourth Pair Of Legs Not With
     Spurious Claws . . . . . . . . . . . . . . . . . . . . . . . .
13a. Eyes Homogeneous . . . . . . . . . . . . . . . . . . . . Araneidae, 114
13b. Eyes Heterogeneous . . . . . . . . . . . . . . . . . . . .
14a. Chelicerae With A Stridulating Organ
     (Fig. 31) . . . . . . . . . . . . . . . . . . . . . . . . . . . Linyphiidae, 101
14b. Chelicerae Without A Stridulating Organ . . . . Theridiosomatidae, 150
15a. All Trochanters Deeply Notched (Fig. 32) . . .
15b. Only Trochanters Of Fourth Pair Of Legs
     Deeply Notched . . . . . . . . . . . . . . . . . . . . . . . Oxyopidae, 218
15c. Trochanters Not Notched . . . . . . . . . . . . . . . . .
16a. Claws Paired With Numerous Teeth . . . . . . . . Pisauridae, 195
16b. Claws Paired With Few Teeth . . . . . . . . . . . . Lycosidae, 200
17a. Tarsi With Trichobothria (Fig. 33) . . . . . . . . Agelenidae, 186
17b. Tarsi Without Trichobothria . . . . . . . . . . . . . . Plectreuridae, 69
18a. Eyes In Two Rows . . . . . . . . . . . . . . . . . . . . . .
18b. Eyes In Three Rows . . . . . . . . . . . . . . . . . . . . .
18c. Eyes In Four Rows . . . . . . . . . . . . . . . . . . . . . Lyssomaniidae, 247
19a. Legs Laterigrade (Fig. 34) . . . . . . . . . . . . . . .
19b. Legs Normal . . . . . . . . . . . . . . . . . . . . . . . . . .
20a. Lower Margin Of Chelicerae With Teeth . . . . Heteropodidae, 170
20b. Lower Margin Of Chelicerae Without Teeth . . Thomisidae, 153
21a. Eyes Homogeneous . . . . . . . . . . . . . . . . . . . . . Clubionidae, 172
21b. Eyes Heterogeneous . . . . . . . . . . . . . . . . . . . . Gnaphosidae, 173
22a. Anterior Median Eyes Smaller Than The
     Lateral Eyes . . . . . . . . . . . . . . . . . . . . . . . . . . Ctenidae, 171
22b. Anterior Median Eyes Larger Than The
     Lateral Eyes . . . . . . . . . . . . . . . . . . . . . . . . . . Salticidae, 220

# 3

# THE FAMILIES OF SPIDERS

## THE FOUR-LUNGED TRUE SPIDERS

*Family Hypochilidae*

The members of this family are doubtless true spiders though they differ from all other spiders and agree with the tarantulas in having two pairs of book lungs. The second pair (Fig. 17) is situated near the middle of the lower surface of the abdomen and the two spiracles are connected by a prominent furrow. There are eight eyes, the anterior median dark, the others pearly white, and the claws of the chelicera are nearly vertical.

*Hypochilus thorelli.* Female ⅗ inch long; male ⅖ inch. Body elongate; legs extremely long and slender, especially the first pair; cribellum a rounded plate; calamistrum, near the base of the fourth metatarsus, of long slender hairs or bristles. General color grayish yellow with irregular dark purplish blotches. Male similar in appearance to the female.

*Hypochilus* prefers dark situations under overhanging rocks and ledges near streams. Here it builds an irregular meshed web shaped like a lampshade, the top pressed against the surface of the overhang.

Mountainous areas of southeastern United States—North Carolina, Kentucky, Tennessee, Georgia and Alabama—where abundant at elevations of from one to about five thousand feet.

## THE ULOBORIDS

*Family  Uloboridae*

The family Uloboridae includes a small number of very remarkable spiders. They have a cribellum and a calamistrum and they spin orb webs but their webs differ from those of the orb weavers in having a hackled band. The eyes are homogeneous, being all dark in color; the lateral eyes on each side are farther apart than are the two pairs of medians. Metatarsi of fourth legs concave above and armed below with a series of spines; calamistrum occupies more than half the length of the segment (Fig. 35).

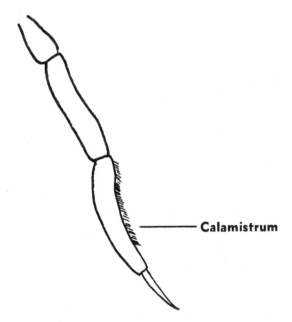

**Fig. 35**
**Metatarsus of Fourth Leg of Uloborus americanus Showing Calamistrum.**

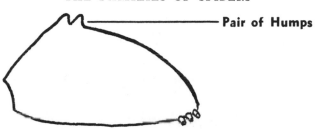

**Pair of Humps**

**Fig. 36**
**Abdomen of Female of Uloborus americanus Showing Pair of Humps.**

*Uloborus americanus, The Featherfoot Spider.* Female about ⅕ inch long; male from ¹⁄₁₀ to ⅛ inch. Cephalothorax oval, longer than wide; abdomen high with a pair of humps at the summit and slightly notched in front (Fig. 36); eyes in two rows; first pair of legs long, the tibia with a brush of long coarse hairs, whence the name of the spider (Fig. 37). Color, various shades of brown, from very light to almost black. The male with a smaller and less distinctly humped abdomen and the tibia of the first pair of legs without the hairs.

The Featherfoot Spider usually occurs in cool shady woods, though sometimes found in buildings, where it spins a horizontal web in

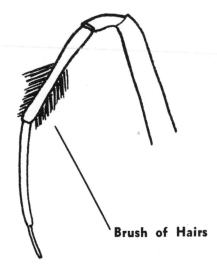

**Brush of Hairs**

**Fig. 37**
**Tibia of First Leg of Uloborus americanus Showing Brush of Hairs.**

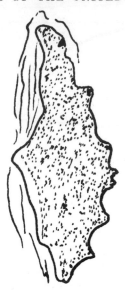

**Fig. 38**
**Egg Sac of Uloborus americanus.**

bushes, the lower branches of trees, or between objects near the ground.

Egg sac elongate, light brown, about one-fourth inch in length, with several tubercles (Fig. 38), and suspended in or near the web.

Widely distributed throughout the United States.

*Hyptiotes cavatus, The Triangle Spider.* Female ⅛ inch long; male about half as long. Cephalothorax wide in the middle, narrow in front, and cut off squarely behind; abdomen oval with four pairs of small elevations on back on which there are a few stiff hairs (Figs. 39 & 39A). Posterior eyes larger than anterior and posterior row longer than anterior (Fig. 40). Legs short. Color brownish gray, the spider in shape and color resembling the ends of branches among which it lives so it is not easily detected. The male with a smaller abdomen and with elevations not as high as those of the female.

The Triangle Spider is usually found in pine woods where it builds its characteristically triangle-shaped web (Fig. 41) among the dead branches of a pine; it is the web that usually calls attention to the spider.

The egg sac which illustrates protective coloration as much as the spider itself is flat, oval and closely attached to the twig. It is about one-fourth inch in length but appears larger because of a sheet-like covering which, gray in color, helps to conceal it.

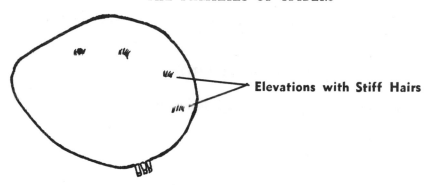

**Fig. 39**
Abdomen of Female of Hyptiotes cavatus. Side View Showing Stiff Hairs.

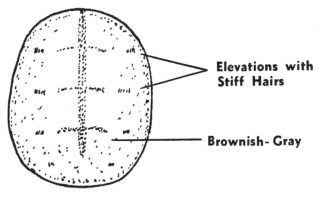

**FIG 39A**
Abdomen of Female of Hyptiotes cavatus. Dorsal View Showing Stiff Hairs.

**Fig. 40**
Head of Hyptiotes cavatus Showing Arrangement of Eyes.

New England south to Georgia and west to the Rocky Mountains.

## THE AMAUROBIIDS

*Family Amaurobiidae*

The spiders of this family are for the most part of average size and all have a cribellum and a calamistrum, the cribellum being divided into two parts and the calamistrum having either a single or double row of curved setae. The eyes are homogeneous, being all light in color; the legs are furnished with strong spines; and the tarsi have three claws.

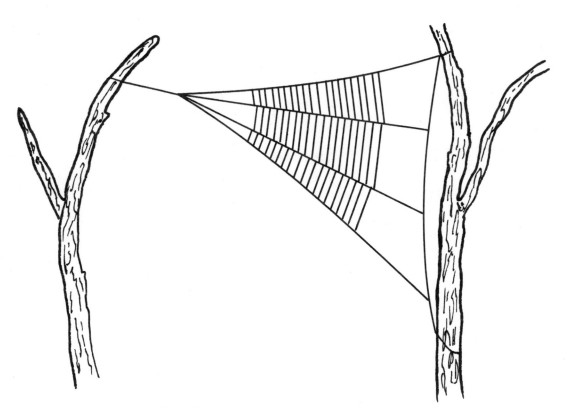

**Fig. 41**
**Web of Triangle Spider, Hyptiotes cavatus.**

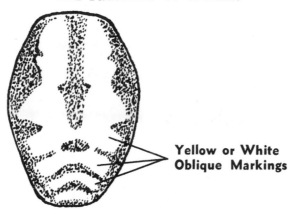

Yellow or White
Oblique Markings

Fig. 42
Amaurobius bennetti.

*Amaurobius bennetti.* Female about ⅖ inch long; male about ⅓ inch. Head of female almost as wide as middle of thorax; abdomen widest behind and usually as long as the cephalothorax or longer. Cephalothorax dark brown; abdomen gray with a double row of oblique yellow or white markings on the hinder half and two curved marks of the same color on the front, the markings sometimes running together so that the entire middle of the abdomen is light colored (Fig. 42).

This is a common spider found under stones and loose bark and in a rock fissure such as a crack in a cliff or cellar wall and prefers cool, moist and poorly lit situations. Its web is an irregular network of threads.

The egg sac is a loosely woven flat sac and covered with an irregular mesh of threads. It is attached to a stone or other object usually near the web.

Occurs throughout the United States.

*Amaurobius ferox.* This is a somewhat larger and darker species than bennetti, and is more domestic in habits, being found in cellars, under floors of dwelling houses, and in debris near human habitations; rarely found far from man.

Common in the eastern United States.

*Titanoeca americana.* About ¼ inch long. Anterior median eyes about same size as posterior medians; calamistrum a single row of bristles. Cephalothorax dull orange color; abdomen black (Fig. 43).

This spider lives under loose stones and dead leaves and prefers areas somewhat drier than those inhabited by *Amaurobius bennetti*.

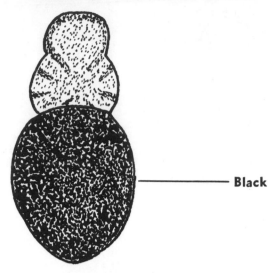

**Fig. 43**
**Titanoeca americana.**

New England south to Georgia and west to Arizona and Utah. *Callioplus tibialis.* Female about ⅓ inch long; male somewhat smaller. Anterior median eyes smaller than posterior medians; calamistrum a single row of curved bristles. Cephalothorax orange or brown; abdomen brown with a lighter median band having scalloped edges (Fig. 44).

Mountain areas from New England to North Carolina.

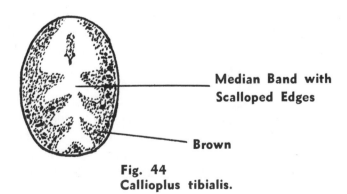

**Fig. 44**
**Callioplus tibialis.**

## THE DICTYNIDS

*Family Dictynidae*

Most of our spiders that have a cribellum and calamistrum belong to this family. They are for the most part small spiders which live on plants, in leaf mold, or under debris on the ground and, not easily frightened, can be seen and observed more readily than many other kinds. Eyes eight in number and heterogeneous, the anterior medians dark, the others pearly white; tarsi with three claws; and fore and hind spinnerets of about the same length. The dictynids spin irregular webs on herbaceous plants and twigs and also on the ground.

*Lathys foxii.* Female $\frac{1}{12}$ inch long; male slightly smaller. Head relatively broad and only slightly elevated; posterior median eyes much larger than anterior medians (Fig. 45). Cephalothorax yellowish; abdomen grayish white with dark gray markings in the form of chevrons (Fig. 46).

This spider spins its webs among dead leaves on the ground and is found more generally in wooded areas.

New England south to Georgia and west to Nebraska.

*Dictyna sublata.* Female $\frac{1}{6}$ inch long; male slightly smaller. Head elevated; anterior median eyes about as large as others; calamistrum covers about half the length of fourth metatarsus. Cephalothorax yellow in front, brown behind; abdomen brown with usually a broad middle yellow band; legs yellow. Male similar to female though there is less color difference in the cephalothorax and the abdomen and legs are darker (Fig. 47).

Web a thin, sheet-like affair spun across the opening of a leaf with slightly rolled edges to form a shallow bed. In leaves of bushes.

Egg sac, as in all species of *Dictyna*, lenticular, white, and attached to web (Fig. 21).

Throughout the United States.

*Dictyna volucripes.* Female about $\frac{1}{6}$ inch long; male somewhat smaller. Head elevated; anterior median eyes about as large as others; calamistrum covers about half the length of fourth metatarsus. Cephalothorax dark brown, partly covered with light gray hairs some of which form three lines extending back from the eyes; abdomen with an elongate dark median band in the front half and irregular pairs of spots in the back half, lighter areas yellowish, and entire abdomen covered with gray hairs, giving the spider the appearance of being clothed in a pleasing gray raiment; legs a lighter brown than cephalothorax and covered with gray hairs (Fig. 48).

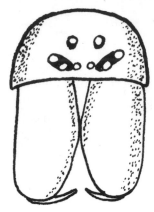

**Fig. 45**
**Face of Lathys foxii Showing Eyes.**

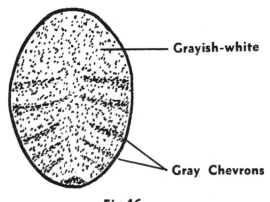

Grayish-white

Gray Chevrons

**Fig.46**
**Lathys foxii.**

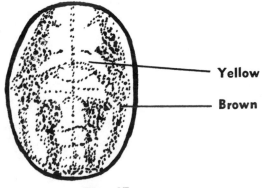

Yellow

Brown

**Fig. 47**
**Dictyna sublata.**

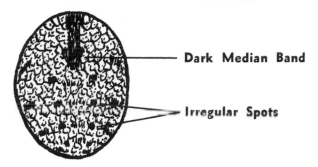

Dark Median Band

Irregular Spots

**Fig. 48**
**Dictyna volucripes.**

Web usually built at the ends of weeds and grasses, preferably the dried stems and stalks left over from the previous growing season, and is a criss-cross of viscid bands woven over foundation lines that are strung from stem to stem to form a lattice network.

Open sunny fields from New England south to Georgia and west to Utah.

*Dictyna foliacea.* Female about ⅛ inch long; male somewhat smaller. Head elevated; anterior median eyes about as large as others; calamistrum covers about half the length of fourth metatarsus. Cephalothorax light brown, darker on the sides, lighter on the head; abdomen yellow in the middle and brown to gray, sometimes red, at the sides, there being a great deal of variation in the width of the central band (Fig. 49). The male differs from the female in that the cephalothorax is bright orange brown without much difference between the head and sides and in that the abdomen is dark reddish brown, sometimes over the entire back but usually with a yellow irregular middle band smaller than that of the female.

This spider lives in grass, bushes, and trees where it builds its web.

New England south to Georgia and west to Nebraska and Oklahoma.

*Dictyna annulipes.* Female about ⅛ inch long; male somewhat smaller. Similar to *volucripes* but somewhat grayer with the band on the front of the abdomen somewhat wider and more broken behind, the dark areas varying greatly in extent.

A favorite site for the web of this spider is a fence or the wall of a building, a tiny crack serving as a retreat from which it can spin out its foundation lines which frequently radiate with considerable regularity and when evenly crossed with the hackled bands form a

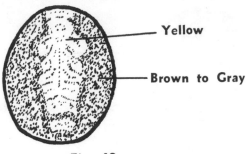

**Fig. 49**
**Dictyna foliacea.**

delicate lacework. Sometimes the spider will select the outside of a
window sash as a site for its snare, when it will be attached to the
smooth glass as well as the wood. The web is also made in grass and
herbaceous plants as well as on the trunks of trees.

Widely distributed throughout the United States.

## THE OECOBIIDS

*Family Oecobiidae*

The spiders of this family are domestic spiders, being found in and
on the walls of buildings; hence the name of the family which is from
the Greek *oikobios,* meaning "living at home." In this family the
cephalothorax is wider than it is long; the cribellum is narrow, trans-

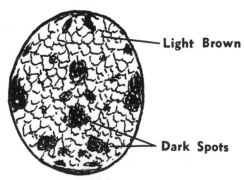

**Fig. 50**
**Oecobius parietalis.**

verse, and divided into two parts; and the calamistrum consists of a double row of bristles and occupies about half the length of the fourth metatarsus. The anterior median eyes and the posterior medians are also triangular or irregular in form.

*Oecobius parietalis.** Female less than ⅛ inch long; the male somewhat smaller. The cephalothorax is pale yellow marked with a marginal black line and spots which are sometimes indistinct or even absent; the abdomen is light brown with dark spots (Fig. 50).

The web, which is about the size of a postage stamp but large enough to capture the tiny insects the spider uses for food, is made over a crack in the side of a building or is stretched over some slightly projecting object. It is a sheet of fine silk and beneath it there is either a tube within which the spider rests or a smaller sheet on which the spider waits for an unwary victim.

New England south to Florida and west to the Pacific Coast; common in the southern part of the United States.

## THE FILISTATIDS

*Family Filistatidae*

This family contains a number of tropical and subtropical species; a few occur in the extreme southern parts of the United States. The cephalothorax of these spiders is oval; the eyes are massed together on a raised prominence (Fig. 51), the anterior median eyes being dark in color and round, the others white and oval or angular; and the calamistrum is near the base of the fourth metatarsus and is very short. Chelicera small and chelate (Fig. 52).

*Filistata hibernalis.* Female from ½ to ⅝ inch long; male somewhat smaller. Female somewhat variable in color, being light brown, dark brown, or sometimes velvety black (Fig. 51). Male a pale yellow with longer legs.

A sedentary spider, *Filistata* lives under stones, in crevices about buildings, and in similar situations. The web is often built on the side of a building around the opening of the spider's retreat and is more or less circular in outline. Sometimes more than a foot in diameter, it is composed of a series of regular radiating lines of dry silk over which is spun many lines of cribellate bands. This sticky silk gathers

---

* Long known as *parietalis*, the spider has been found to be identical with the universally distributed *annulipes* and probably should now go under this name.

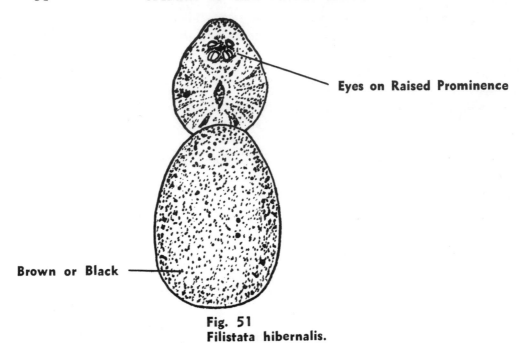

Eyes on Raised Prominence

Brown or Black

**Fig. 51**
**Filistata hibernalis.**

dust and other debris so that eventually accumulations of such material make the web quite conspicuous.

A very common house spider in the southern states west to California.

## THE DYSDERIDS

*Family Dysderidae*

This is a small family of six-eyed spiders with two tarsal claws and claw tufts and four conspicuous spiracles near the base of the abdomen, two leading to the book lungs and the others to the air-tubes. *Dysdera crocata.* About half an inch long. Abdomen a little longer than the cephalothorax; six eyes close together on front (Fig. 53) of head; coxae of first two pairs of legs cylindrical, longer and thinner than last two pairs. Cephalothorax and legs orange brown; abdomen same color but so pale as to be almost white (Fig. 54).

This spider lives under stones but at times also under bark and in moss, usually in places that are dark and humid. An oval cell of closely

**Fig. 52**
**Eyes and Chelicera of Filistata.**

**Fig. 53**
**Dysdera crocata. Head Showing Arrangement of Eyes.**

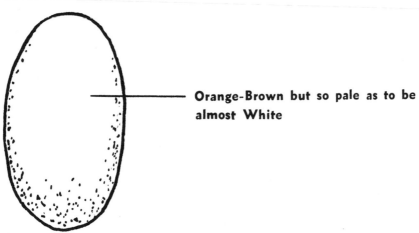

Orange-Brown but so pale as to be almost White

**Fig. 54**
**Dysdera crocata.**

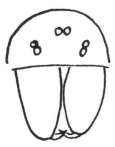

**Fig. 55**
**Ariadna bicolor. Face Showing Arrangement of Eyes.**

woven silk provides a retreat and within it the eggs are placed without any special covering.

Usually found near buildings from New England south to Georgia and west to Nebraska.

## THE SEGESTRIIDS

*Family Segestriidae*

The spiders of this family are somewhat cylindrical in form with six eyes in three groups of two each (Fig. 55), the tarsi with three claws, and four spiracles near the base of the abdomen, the posterior

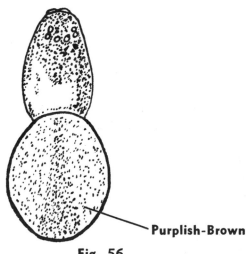

Purplish-Brown

**Fig. 56**
**Ariadna tricolor.**

pair the openings to the air tubes. The first three pairs of legs are directed forward and the first two pairs with which the spiders hold their victims are armed below with numerous stout spines.

*Ariadna bicolor.* About ⅓ inch long. Cephalothorax yellow brown, relatively long and narrow; abdomen purplish-brown and a long oval; legs yellow brown (Fig. 56).

This spider builds a tubular retreat, in which it sits with its first six legs directed forward in a position to leap, in a crack or otherwise suitable crevice in a tree, rock or some similar place. The retreat is suspended from a framework of threads and is continued outside and around the mouth opening as a silken collar. From the inner edge of the mouth a series of radiating lines extend outward like the spokes of a wheel and are attached by little silken piers above the surface of the substratum. When one of these lines is touched by an unwary insect the effect is to bring out the spider with incredible swiftness to the spot where the insect has tripped the silken thread. The spider then backs into the tube carrying the insect with it.

Found almost everywhere throughout the United States.

## THE OONOPIDS

*Family Oonopidae*

The oonopids are small spiders, most of them less than ⅙ inch long, and live in leaf mold or under stones. They have six eyes and four spiracles but the tracheal spiracles are inconspicuous.

*Orchestina saltitans.* Less than ¹⁄₂₀ inch long. Median eyes widely separated, the anterior lateral eyes forming with them a straight transverse row (Fig. 57). Cephalothorax convex, highest in the middle, yellow or whitish with purplish markings and a black marginal line and a black spot around the eyes; abdomen purplish with many long fine hairs (Fig. 58).

Occurs in grass and on bushes but found most commonly inside

**Fig. 57**
**Orchestina saltitans. Head Showing Arrangement of Eyes.**

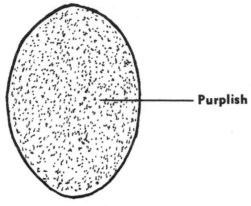

**Fig. 58**
**Orchestina saltitans.**

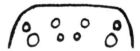

**Fig. 59**
**Plectreurys tristis. Head Showing Arrangement of Eyes.**

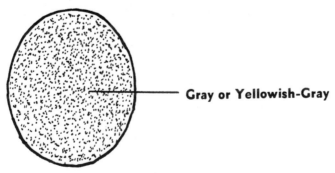

**Fig. 60**
**Plectreurys tristis.**

buildings where it may often be seen moving slowly over tables, among books on a desk, or hanging by its threads from a lampshade. It has a marked jumping ability, due to the unusual development of the hind femora, and can be induced to jump by touching it gently.

New England south to Georgia and west to the Mississippi.

## THE PLECTREURIDIDS

*Family Plectreuridae*

The plectreuridids are eight-eyed, three-clawed spiders that live under stones in our southwestern deserts. The eyes are placed in two essentially straight rows, the anterior median eyes being smaller and somewhat nearer the lateral eyes (Fig. 59). The legs are stout and in the males the first pair of legs has a stout spur at the end of the tibia. *Plectreurys tristis.* About ½ inch long. Cephalothorax and legs dark brown; abdomen gray or yellowish-gray with gray pubescence (Fig. 60).

Utah, Arizona, to California.

## THE DIGUETIDS

*Family Diguetidae*

The members of this family are six-eyed, three-clawed rather elongated spiders with the anterior eyes in a nearly straight line and with their bodies thickly covered with white hairs.
*Diguetia canities.* About ⅜ inch long. Cephalothorax orange or tan; abdomen much the same color; both thickly covered with white pubescence; abdomen also with a white-bordered folium (Fig. 60A). Legs yellow and ringed with brown or black bands.

The spider spins a long vertical retreat, as much as three or four inches long and closed at the top which it suspends in the center of a maze of threads, a favorite site being the space between the joints of prickly pear and small bush cacti. The egg sacs are incorporated within the tube, being laid one upon another like the tiles of a roof.

Southern Rocky Mountain states west to California.

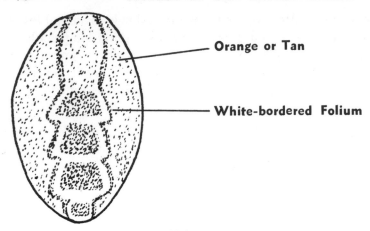

Orange or Tan

White-bordered Folium

**Fig. 60A**
**Diguetia canities.**

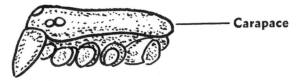

Carapace

**Fig. 61**
**Loxosceles unicolor. Cephalothorax Showing Flat Carapace.**

**Fig. 62**
**Loxosceles unicolor. Head Showing Arrangement of Eyes.**

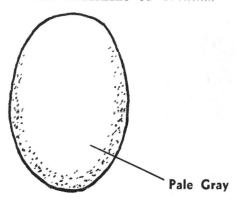

**Fig. 63**
**Loxosceles unicolor.**

## THE LOXOSCELIDS

*Family Loxoscelidae*

The loxoscelids are medium-size spiders with six eyes and two tarsal claws. The carapace is flat above (Fig. 61), the thoracic furrow conspicuous and longitudinal, the anterior row of eyes (Fig. 62) is recurved, and the legs are long.

*Loxosceles unicolor.* Female about $\frac{5}{16}$ inch long; male about ¼ inch. Cephalothorax light orange yellow with slight pubescence; abdomen pale gray with (Fig. 63) a few hairs; legs same color as cephalothorax but darker distally. An unusual feature of this spider is the presence of a large and conspicuous colulus (Fig. 64).

Loxosceles lives under stones on the ground and under the bark of trees and weaves a large, irregular web, the threads being like those of the hackled band weavers.

Oklahoma and Texas west to California.

*Loxosceles reclusus. The Brown Recluse Spider.* About ½ inch long.

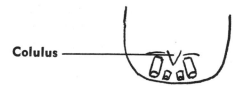

**Fig. 64**
**Loxosceles unicolor. Tip of Abdomen Showing Colulus.**

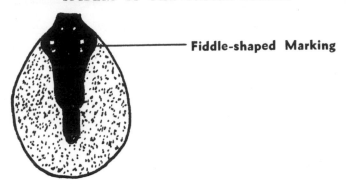

Fiddle-shaped Marking

**Fig. 65**
**Loxosceles reclusa.**

Cephalothorax light colored with a dark fiddle-shaped marking; abdomen brown; legs brown (Fig. 65).

This spider, whose bite is considered dangerous though reactions to the bite may range from mild to severe, is found outdoors under rocks and bark as well as indoors in houses, schools, sheds, and barns. During the day it remains in some quiet place as in a closet, beneath furniture, or in any kind of receptacle, coming out at night to search for food.

South Central states.

## THE SCYTODIDS

*Family Scytodidae*

The Scytodids are of small or medium size, rather attractive in appearance, and tinted in pale yellow or white and ornamented with black or gray spots. They are six-eyed and three-clawed, with a cephalothorax that is oval and quite elevated (Fig. 66), sometimes nearly globose, an oval abdomen, and legs that are very long and thin. Nocturnal in habit, they live under stones, in rock fissures, in buildings, and on the leaves of plants where they spin a thin, flat web. Several species occur in the southern states but the following species has a more northern distribution.

*Scytodes thoracica. The Spitting Spider.* About ¼ inch long. Cephalothorax and abdomen yellow with black markings (Fig. 67).

This spider is a domestic species and is most often observed in

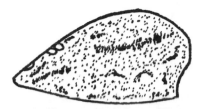

**Fig. 66**
**Scytodes thoracia. Side View of Cephalothorax.**

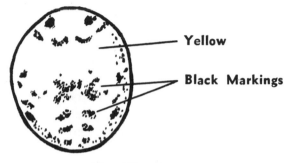

Yellow

Black Markings

**Fig. 67**
**Scytodes thoracia.**

shaded corners and dark closets or walking leisurely over the walls and ceilings of houses at night in search of small prey. When one is discovered it ejects a viscous secretion from its chelicerae in which the victim is entangled and stuck to the substratum, the entire procedure being practically instantaneous. The secretion is produced in the venom glands which are also capable of secreting an adequate quantity of venom.

Eastern States westward to Indiana.

## THE GNAPHOSIDS

*Family Gnaphosidae*

The gnaphosids are mostly ground spiders and rather drab and somber in appearance with few contrasting markings though some are brightly colored. They have eight eyes, arranged in two rows, and which are heterogeneous, the anterior medians (Fig. 68) dark; two tarsal claws, the tarsus with bundles of terminal tenent hairs (claw

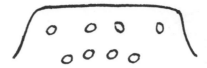

**Fig. 68**
**Gnaphosa muscorum. Head Showing Arrangement of Eyes.**

tufts), and an abdomen that is oval and usually flattened. They are generally two or three times as long as wide and the anterior spinnerets are cylindrical and longer than the posterior. Most species are found under stones or bark or in moss though a few live on the leaves of plants which they roll but they do not build a definite tube; at the most they spin an irregular retreat at the time of egg-laying. Some of the species that live beneath stones spin a silken sac within which they live and in which they place the egg sac.

*Drassodes neglectus.* Female nearly ½ inch long; male smaller and more slender. Posterior median eyes oval, oblique and closer to each other than to the laterals (Fig. 69). Cephalothorax and abdomen yellow to light gray with an indistinct longitudinal stripe on the anterior part of the abdomen, faint chevrons on the posterior part (Fig. 70), and four spots on the muscle depressions.

This is one of the more common members of the family. It lives under stones and other objects on the ground where it makes a large transparent bag of silk in which it lives and within which the egg sac is made.

New England west to Oklahoma and the Pacific Coast.

*Haplodrassus signifer.* Female from ⅓ to nearly ½ inch long; male much smaller. Anterior median eyes larger than the anterior laterals; posterior medians large and oblique and set close together away from the lateral eyes (Fig. 71). Carapace and legs yellowish orange; abdomen gray.

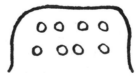

**Fig. 69**
**Drassodes neglectus. Head Showing Arrangement of Eyes.**

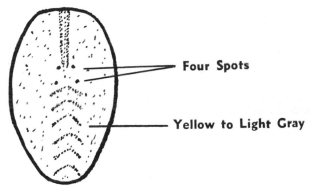

Four Spots

Yellow to Light Gray

**Fig. 70**
**Drassodes neglectus.**

Lives under stones and other objects in fields and pastures.

Throughout the northern states.

*Orodrassus coloradensis.* Female about ½ inch long; male slightly smaller. Posterior median eyes circular and smaller than anterior medians. Cephalothorax orange to brown; abdomen gray to brown.

Canadian border south to Arizona.

*Poecilochroa montana.* Female about ⅓ inch long; male about ⅕ inch. Cephalothorax narrow, oblong, slightly convex and somewhat narrowed in front. Anterior median eyes larger than posterior medians and close together in a straight line. Cephalothorax dark brown covered with a few white hairs; abdomen black with a pair of white spots across the middle and a white band across the front end; legs dark brown (Fig. 72).

Across the northern states from New England to the Pacific Coast.

*Poecilochroa variegata.* Female ¼ inch long; male smaller. Cephalothorax bright orange, somewhat darker towards the eyes; abdomen black with three transverse white stripes and a T–shaped white mark between the first and second stripes; legs orange with the femora of the first and second pairs black. An easily recognised species because of its abdominal markings (Fig. 73).

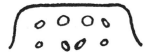

**Fig. 71**
**Haplodrassus signifer. Head Showing Arrangement of Eyes.**

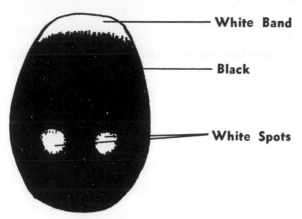

White Band

Black

White Spots

**Fig. 72**
**Poecilochroa montana.**

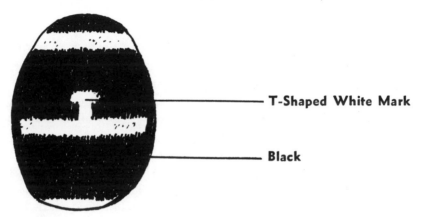

T-Shaped White Mark

Black

**Fig. 73**
**Poecilochroa variegata.**

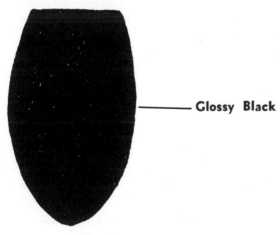

Glossy Black

**Fig. 74**
**Zelotes subterraneus.**

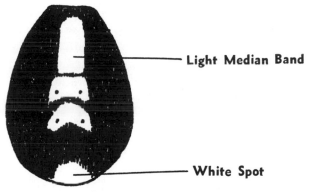

Light Median Band

White Spot

**Fig. 75**
**Herpyllus vasifer.**

Found under stones and dead leaves in woods.

Widely distributed throughout the East from New England south to Georgia and west to Nebraska and Oklahoma.

*Zelotes subterraneus.* Female nearly ⅓ inch long; male about the same. Cephalothorax ovate or egg-shaped, very much narrowed in front; anterior eyes near together in a procurved line, posterior eyes in a straight or nearly straight line. Cephalothorax and abdomen a glossy black (Fig. 74).

Found under stones and dead leaves.

Common and widely distributed throughout the northern states.

*Drassyllus rufulus.* Female about ¼ inch long; male about the same. Posterior row of eyes procurved, medians close together and larger than lateral eyes. Cephalothorax light reddish-brown without markings; abdomen paler.

Occurs under stones to which the egg sac is attached; it consists of two circular sheets of silk the eggs being placed between them. Sometimes the outer sheet becomes so covered with dirt or mud that it resembles the stones.

Distributed generally throughout the East.

*Note:* Two other species common throughout the East are *Drassyllus frigidus* and *Drassyllus depressus.* The male and female of *D. frigidus* are a little less than ⅕ of an inch long; the cephalothorax is brownish-yellow with a black margin; and the abdomen is blackish with the body covered with black hairs. The female of *D. depressus* is about ¼ inch long, the male somewhat less. The cephalothorax is orange to dark brown; the abdomen gray to black without markings. Both are found under stones, leaves, and logs on the ground.

*Herpyllus vasifer.* Female ⅓ inch long; male much smaller. Two rows of eyes nearly straight, rows widely separated, and eyes of each row evenly spaced, anterior median eyes larger than the others and posterior medians smaller than posterior laterals. Cephalothorax dull black at the sides with a whitish stripe in the middle; abdomen black with a light median band that extends from the basal end for about two-thirds of its length and a white spot at the posterior end; legs dull black (Fig. 75).

Lives under stones, rubbish, and other objects on the ground, between boards, and in crevices in dark places. Runs rapidly when disturbed.

The egg sac is flat and snowy-white.

New England south to Georgia and west to Oklahoma and Colorado.

*Litopyllus rupicolens.* Female ⅓ inch long; male somewhat smaller. Median eyes of posterior row much larger than the laterals, nearer together, row rather strongly procurved. Cephalothorax yellowish-brown; abdomen nearly uniform gray; legs yellowish-brown.

Eastern United States.

*Cesonia bilineata.* Female about ¼ inch long; male somewhat smaller.

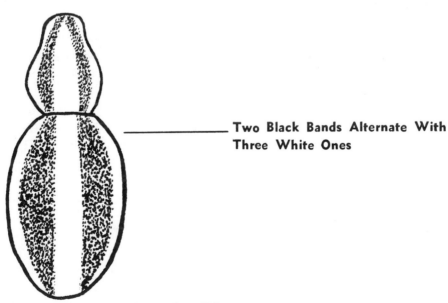

Two Black Bands Alternate With
Three White Ones

Fig. 76
Cesonia bilineata.

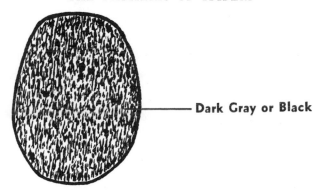

Dark Gray or Black

**Fig. 77**
**Gnaphosa muscorum.**

Cephalothorax low and narrowed in front. The two rows of eyes are nearly straight and widely separated, median eyes of each row farther apart than they are from the lateral eyes. This is an easily recognized spider because two black bands which alternate with three white ones run the entire length of both the cephalothorax and abdomen (Fig. 76); legs gray with white hairs.

Found under stones and leaves in wooded areas.

Egg sac snowy-white and flat and attached to the lower surface of a stone.

Atlantic coast west to Nebraska.

*Gnaphosa muscorum.* Female about ½ inch long; male slightly less. Posterior eye row much longer than anterior, median eyes nearer to each other than to the laterals. Cephalothorax dark brown with black markings along radial furrows. Abdomen dark gray or black, covered with fine hairs (Fig. 77).

Found under stones in fields and pastures and beneath logs in woodlands.

New England west to the Pacific Coast.

*Gnaphosa sericata.* Female about ¼ inch long; male slightly smaller; Cephalothorax yellowish-red or brownish-red to orange; abdomen bluish-black or gray to black. Eyes similar to *muscorum.*

Found under stones and leaves.

A common southern species, Long Island south to Florida and west to Texas and Colorado.

*Callilepsis imbecilla.* Female about ¼ inch long; male about the same or slightly smaller. Posterior row of eyes but little longer than the anterior and straight or only slightly recurved. Posterior laterals larger than posterior medians. Cephalothorax orange or bright orange-brown; abdomen bluish-black with white hairs around the muscle-impressions (Fig. 78).

A very active spider living under stones in fields and pastures where it spins a slight irregular web.

Egg sac plano-convex and white.

Throughout the United States.

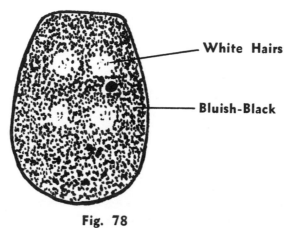

**Fig. 78**
**Callilepsis imbecilla.**

## THE PHOLCIDS

*Family Pholcidae*

The pholcids are spiders with elongate or spherical bodies and such long thin legs that they are sometimes mistaken for the harvestmen or daddy-longlegs (Fig. 79). The tarsi are flexible with three claws and the anterior median eyes are the smallest. They spin webs which are either sheet-like or irregular in dark places and in which they hang with the back downward. The males live in the same webs as the females and resemble them closely but may be distinguished from them by the size of the palpi which are enlarged to form thickened appendages. The females carry the eggs, which are glued to-

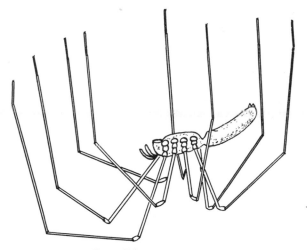

**Fig. 79**
**Pholcus phalangiodes.**

gether in a spherical mass and tied lightly with a few threads, in their chelicerae and when the eggs hatch the females may be observed holding the spiderlings. Many of the pholcids, especially in the south-western states, have become domestic in habit.

*Spermophora meridionalis.* Female about ½ inch long; male slightly smaller. Six eyes, in two pairs of three each (Fig. 80), anterior medians being absent. Entire body pale yellow or (Fig. 81) white with a pair of pale gray spots on the thorax; abdomen globose.

This is a house spider, living in dark places such as corners and closets and under furniture.

Eastern United States west to Missouri.

*Pholcus phalangiodes. The Long-legged Cellar Spider.* Female ¼ inch long; male slightly smaller. Abdomen elongate, about three times as long as wide and more than twice as long as the cephalothorax which is nearly round; eight eyes, anterior medians closer to each other than to anterior laterals. Color of body pale yellow or pale brown with a gray patch in the center of carapace (Fig. 79).

This is a very common spider living in cellars where there is little light and spinning a very large loose web.

Throughout the United States.

*Physocyclus globosus.* Female about ⅙ inch long; male somewhat smaller. Posterior row of eyes slightly recurved, anterior medians farther removed from posterior medians than from anterior laterals,

**Fig. 80**
**Spermophora meridionalis. Head Showing Arrangement of Eyes.**

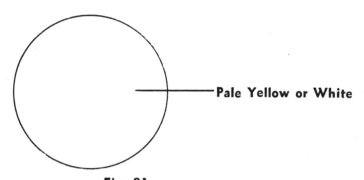

Pale Yellow or White

**Fig. 81**
**Spermophora meridionalis.**

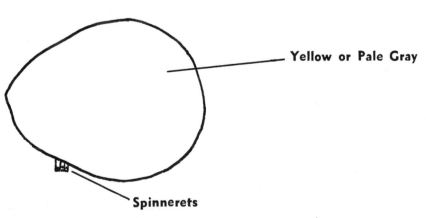

Yellow or Pale Gray

Spinnerets

**Fig. 82**
**Psilochorus pullulus.**

anterior laterals slightly larger than posterior medians; cephalothorax broader than long; abdomen as high as long and appearing triangular in profile; cephalothorax yellow with a brownish middle line; abdomen yellow-brown or gray with many small black flecks; legs light yellow with darker rings at distal ends of femora and both ends of tibiae.

A house spider occurring from Florida to California.

*Psilochorus pullulus.* Female about ⅒ inch long; male slightly smaller. Abdomen greatly arched and projecting far beyond the spinnerets; eight eyes, posterior row slightly procurved, the medians slightly the larger, and larger than the anterior laterals. Cephalothorax yellowish with a forked black mark along thoracic groove; eyes surrounded with black; abdomen yellow or pale gray and often marked with green or greenish-purple spots; legs yellow (Fig. 82).

Lives in dark places where it spins a somewhat small, tangled mass of threads.

Maryland south to Georgia and west to Nebraska and Arizona.

## THE COMB-FOOTED SPIDERS

*Family Theridiidae*

The members of this family are called the comb-footed spiders because they have on the tarsus of the fourth pair of legs a distinct comb consisting of a row of strong, curved, and toothed setae or bristles (Fig. 30). Usually the comb is quite apparent but in some species it is difficult to see and in a few others it has been reduced to a small number of modified setae. It is used to fling silk over the prey. The spiders have eight eyes and three tarsal claws and, with some

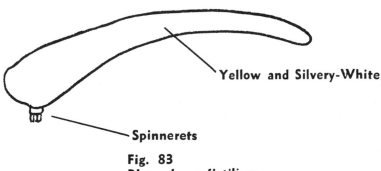

Yellow and Silvery-White

Spinnerets

Fig. 83
Rhomphaea fictilium.

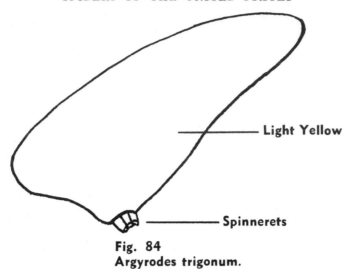

**Fig. 84**
**Argyrodes trigonum.**

exceptions, are sedentary in habits, spinning webs with which to trap their prey and in which to place their egg sacs. The webs are composed of threads extending in all directions without any regular plan and in them the spiders hang upside down. While some species live in houses where they spin their webs in corners, others live outdoors and spin their snares in fences, among rocks, and between the branches and leaves of low trees and bushes.

*Rhomphaea fictilium.* Female about ⅓ inch long; male somewhat smaller. Abdomen long, slender, and wormlike; cephalothorax with a deep transverse furrow near the middle; legs very long and slender; lateral eyes of each side close together, medians widely separated, those of each side being near to the laterals forming a group of four eyes on each side. Light yellow and silvery white in color, with three darker bands on the cephalothorax and one on the middle of the abdomen (Fig. 83).

This spider spins a tiny web between the leaves of bushes or blades of grass.

The egg sac is yellowish, shaped like a vase, and about the same size as the spider.

Throughout the United States.

*Argyrodes (Conopistha) trigona.* Female ⅛ inch from head to spinnerets and about as much from spinnerets to tip of abdomen; male smaller than female. Abdomen high, pointed and triangular when seen from the side (Fig. 84); cephalothorax with a transverse furrow

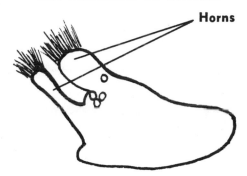

**Horns**

**Fig. 85**
**Argyrodes trigonum. Cephalothorax of Male Showing Horns.**

across the middle; the part of the head bearing the eyes slightly raised. Color light yellow, sometimes with a metallic luster, cephalothorax with three light brown stripes and abdomen at times with dark spots at the sides. Male darker colored, with a smaller and less angular abdomen, and easily recognized by the two projecting horns on the head, each tipped by a bunch of toothed hairs (Fig. 85).

The web is built among the branches of shrubs but quite frequently the spider is found in the web of some other spider with which it lives as a commensal, feeding on the smaller insects caught in the web but ignored by its host. The form and color of the spider gives it a degree of protection since it resembles the scale of a bud caught in the web.

The egg sac is a beautiful vase-shaped object and when first made is white in color but later changes to a brown. It is suspended by a thread in the web (Fig. 24).

Occurs all over the United States.

*Argyrodes (Conopistha) nephilae.* The spider resembles *trigona* in size and having a triangular abdomen but differs in appearance in that a large part of the upper abdomen is silver-white so that it looks much like a drop of quicksilver. Cephalothorax is dark brown or black and the lower side of the abdomen is black.

This species also resembles *trigona* in habits living both an independent existence and as a commensal in the webs of larger spiders, especially in the webs of the silk spider *Nephila* which suggested its specific name.

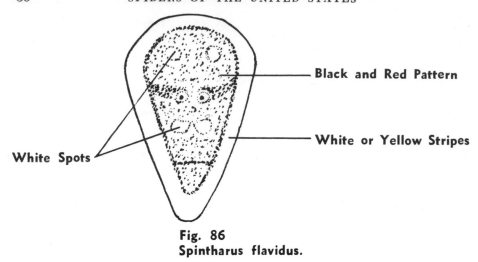

Fig. 86
Spintharus flavidus.

Distributed throughout the southern states from the Atlantic to the Pacific.

*Spintharus flavidus.* Female from ⅙ to ¼ inch long; male about ⅛ inch. Lateral eyes of each side contiguous, posterior medians widely separated being three or four times the diameter of one of them apart. Cephalothorax yellow; abdomen reddish-brown with a white or yellow stripe on each side, on the upper surface between these stripes is a pattern in black and red lighter toward the middle where there are two or three pairs of white spots (Fig. 86); legs yellow. Pattern

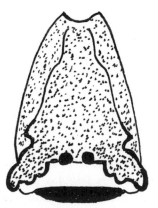

Fig. 86A
Episinus amoenus.

on upper surface of abdomen varies in individuals. Male with longer legs and a more slender abdomen and also varies in markings.

A common species on the lower surface of leaves of bushes. At a glance it appears to be resting on the leaf but a closer scrutiny shows that each foot is supported by a thread.

New England south to Florida and west to Oklahoma.

*Episinus amoenus.* Female about ⅛ inch long; male ⅒ inch. This spider is easily recognized by the form of its abdomen which is narrow and bi-lobed at the base, gradually widening towards the posterior end; a tubercle on each side of the abdomen at its widest part the abdomen thereafter tapering to a point (Fig. 86A).

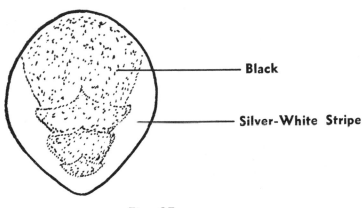

— Black

— Silver-White Stripe

**Fig. 87**
**Euryopis funebris.**

Found on bushes, in habits resembling those of Spintharus.

Southeastern states.

*Euryopis funebris.* Female about ⅛ inch long; male about the same or slightly smaller. Anterior median eyes much larger and much wider apart than posterior medians; abdomen pointed behind, heart-shaped. General color black or dark gray; abdomen bordered with a silver white stripe (Fig. 87) on the posterior half and within this stripe the upper surface is black, broken by light spots in the middle.

Found on bushes in the summer and beneath dead leaves on the ground in winter.

A common and widely distributed species, occurring over most of the United States.

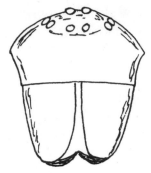

**Fig. 88**
**Theridion tepidariorum. Face Showing Eyes and Chelicerae.**

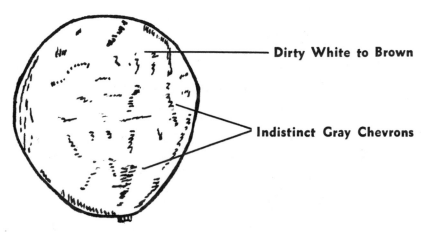

Dirty White to Brown

Indistinct Gray Chevrons

**Fig. 89**
**Theridion tepidariorum. Side View of Abdomen of Female.**

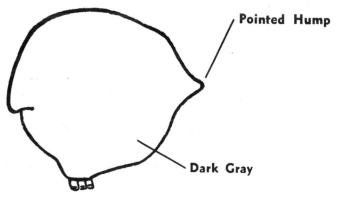

Pointed Hump

Dark Gray

**Fig. 90**
**Theridion rupicola.**

*Note:* A somewhat larger species is *Euryopis scriptipes* and rather similar in appearance except that the silvery margin on the abdomen completely surrounds an irregular, triangular dark spot in the middle of the back.

*Theridion tepidariorum. The Domestic Spider.* Female ¼ inch long or slightly more; male somewhat smaller. Lateral eyes of each side contiguous (Fig. 88); abdomen high in front and narrows towards the spinnerets; first pair of legs nearly three times the length of the body. Cephalothorax yellowish-brown; abdomen dirty white to brown with indistinct gray chevrons on posterior half; legs yellow with brown or gray rings at the end of the segments (Fig. 89).

This is an extremely common spider and though it may be found outdoors under stones and boards and on fences and bridges it is more commonly seen in houses and barns where its tangle of threads may be found in the corners of rooms and the angles of windows.

The egg sac is brownish, usually pear-shaped, with a tough papery cover and is suspended in the web.

Throughout the United States.

*Theridion rupicola.* Female about ⅒ inch long; male about ¹⁄₁₂ inch. Abdomen with a pointed hump which is about midway between the base of the abdomen and the spinnerets which makes this species easy to recognize. General color dark gray with darker gray and brownish markings (Fig. 90).

Lives under stones in woods and under boards and rubbish around houses where it spins a web that often contains grains of sand or debris and in which it hides its disk-like white to brown egg sac.

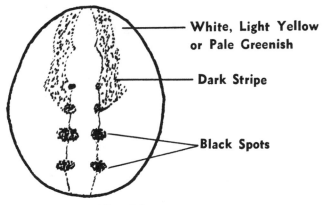

**White, Light Yellow or Pale Greenish**

**Dark Stripe**

**Black Spots**

**Fig. 91
Theridion frondeum.**

New England south to Alabama and west to the Pacific Coast.

*Theridion frondeum.* Female from ⅛ to ⅙ inch long; male ⅛ inch. Front legs long, those of the female from ⅓ to ⅖ inch, of the male the same length. General color white, light yellow, or pale greenish with dark markings that vary considerably, in fact this species is so variable in its markings (Fig. 91) that a number of individuals may represent half as many species. Cephalothorax may have a narrow or broad dark band down the center and the abdomen may have several dusky bands, or dark stripes, and small black spots; legs white with dark spots at ends of segments.

This spider, which frequently attracts attention because of its conspicuous colors, is one of the more common species found in fields where it spins its web on the under side of leaves in bushes and also in tall grass.

The egg sac is spherical, snowy-white in color, and loose in texture and is fastened in the web.

New England south to Alabama and west to the Pacific.

*Theridion (Henziectypus) globosum.* Female about ⅛ inch long; male somewhat smaller. Abdomen high, flattened behind and pointed towards the spinnerets. Cephalothorax orange-brown except a black spot between the eyes; abdomen yellowish-gray on anterior upper part, posterior part white with a black spot in the middle; legs orange-brown (Fig. 92).

Occurs in leaf litter, in holes of tree stumps, and similar places.

Egg sac cream-colored, lozenge-shaped, and pointed at both ends.

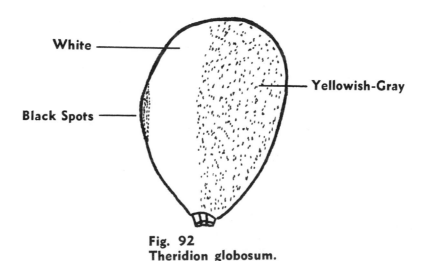

Fig. 92
Theridion globosum.

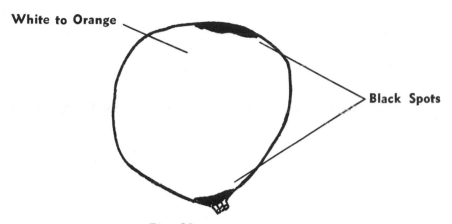

White to Orange

Black Spots

**Fig. 93**
**Theridion unimaculatum.**

Maine south to Florida and west to Illinois.

*Theridion unimaculatum.* Female about $\frac{1}{12}$ inch long; male somewhat smaller. Abdomen oval. Cephalothorax orange with a black spot around the eyes; abdomen white to orange with a black spot in the center of the back and a black ring around the spinnerets by which it can easily be recognized; legs orange (Fig. 93).

Lives among leaves of bushes and low plants where it spins its web.

Maine to Florida and west to Illinois.

*Theridion differens.* Female about $\frac{1}{8}$ inch long; male smaller. Cephalothorax orange-brown, often darker in the middle; abdomen round

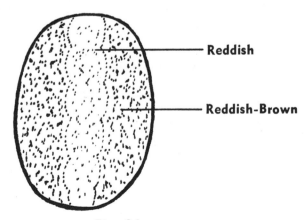

Reddish

Reddish-Brown

**Fig. 94**
**Theridion differens.**

with a median stripe often very brightly colored with white or yellow at the edges and red in the center, rest of abdomen reddish-brown. In the male the stripe on the abdomen is obscure and the entire abdomen is dark reddish-brown; legs yellow in female and orange-brown in male (Fig. 94).

Web on low plants of all kinds and consists of a small tent, barely large enough to cover the spider, from which an irregular network of threads spreads out over the plant.

Egg sac white, nearly as large as the spider, and attached to the web.

Generally throughout the East.

*Theridion murarium.* Female about ⅛ inch long; male about the same or slightly smaller. Abdomen nearly spherical. Cephalothorax grayish-yellow with a narrow black marginal stripe each side and a wider median stripe which is sometimes divided near the eyes; abdomen with a wavy middle stripe, white at the edges and reddish in the center, and gray to black on either side of the band (Fig. 95).

Web spun in trees, in bushes and grass, as well as beneath stones.

Egg sac spherical, white to tan, and attached in the web.

Maine south to Alabama and west to the Pacific.

*Theridion (Anelosimus) studiosum.* Female ⅙ inch long; male nearly ⅛ inch. Cephalothorax reddish-yellow with an indistinct median band extending forward from the dorsal groove and forking to send two branches to the eyes; abdomen greenish-brown to brownish-gray on the sides with a dark median band bordered in white (Fig. 95A).

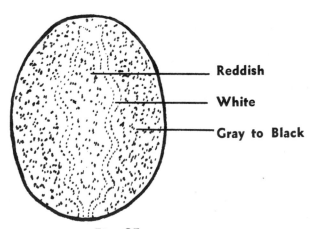

Reddish

White

Gray to Black

**Fig. 95**
**Theridion murarium.**

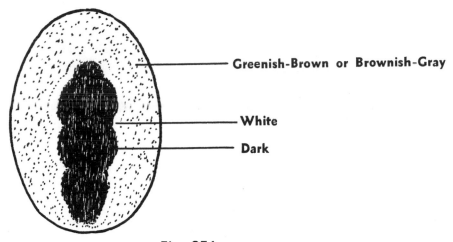

Greenish-Brown or Brownish-Gray

White

Dark

**Fig. 95A**
**Theridion studiosum.**

An interesting and unusual spider because of its social habits, colony formation being rare among spiders. Its communal web is placed on shrubs and trees and usually consists of an unsightly mass of dead leaves tied together with silk and serving as a retreat, a sheet of silk attached to twigs surrounding it. Several spiders live together in the nests. (A South American species, *Anelosimus eximius,* lives in even larger colonies, as many as hundreds or even thousands of individuals living together in a common web.)

New England south to Florida and west to California.

*Theridion spirale.* About the same size as *T. differens.* Cephalothorax orange-brown with an indistinct dark stripe as wide in front as the eyes and narrowed behind; abdomen gray with a middle stripe usually gray but sometimes reddish; legs pale, sometimes with faint gray rings at the ends and middle of each segment.

Throughout the East.

*Theridula opulenta.* Female about ¹⁄₁₀ of an inch long; male about the same, Anterior row of eyes procurved, posterior medians slightly larger than posterior laterals; abdomen in female wider than long with a hump at each side in the middle of its length. Cephalothorax yellow or yellowish-gray with a conspicuous broad, dark band in the middle; abdomen yellowish-gray with a white spot in the middle with a black spot on a slight elevation on each side and around the spinnerets; legs light yellow. In the male the cephalothorax and legs are orange and the markings of the abdomen less distinct (Fig. 96).

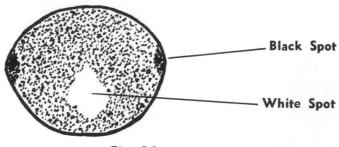

**Fig. 96**
**Theridula opulenta.**

Lives on bushes.

Throughout the United States.

*Dipoena nigra.* Female about ⅒ inch long; male slightly smaller. Anterior eyes larger and much wider apart than the posterior medians; abdomen oval and rounded behind. Cephalothorax yellow to brown; abdomen black; legs same color as cephalothorax (Fig. 97).

Irregular web on bushes or on the low branches of trees, especially conifers.

Maine south to Florida and west to Arizona.

*Note:* Three other species are found in the United States. They are *D. lascivula,* abdomen light yellow; *D. buccalis,* abdomen light brown; and *D. crassiventris,* abdomen dark brownish-gray. Female of *lascivula* ¹⁄₁₂ inch long, of *buccalis* ⅕ inch, and of *crassiventris* ⅐ inch.

**Fig. 97**
**Dipoena nigra.**

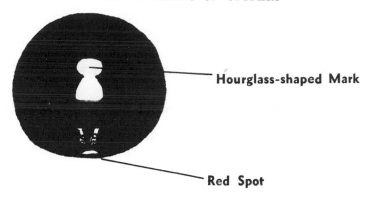

Hourglass-shaped Mark

Red Spot

**Fig. 97A**
**Latrodectus mactans.**

*Latrodectus mactans. The Black Widow.* Female about ½ inch long; male about ¼ inch. Lateral eyes of each side widely separated; abdomen globose. This is a coal black spider with markings of red or yellow or both which vary greatly. Typically there is an hourglass-shaped mark on the lower surface of the abdomen (Fig. 97A). There is also more commonly a single red spot just behind the spinnerets and sometimes a row along the back but they may vary in number and be wanting altogether. The male is more conspicuously marked than the female, having, in addition to the marks of the female, four white stripes along the sides of the abdomen. This spider is subject to considerable variation in coloration and several geographic races or forms may be found throughout the country, the southern and western forms being more strikingly marked than the northern and eastern ones.

The black widow is a shy sedentary species, largely nocturnal in habits, and seldom leaves its silken home. The web is an irregular mesh usually built quite close to the ground with a strong-walled funnel-shaped retreat and is usually built under stones or logs, about stumps, in holes in the ground and in barns and other outbuildings.

The egg sac is pear-shaped to almost globular in form, white to tan, and of a tough papery texture.

Found in every state but more common and abundant in the south and west.

*Crustulina guttata.* Female about ¹⁄₁₀ inch long; male the same size. Cephalothorax conspicuously marked with many small crescent-shaped elevations each at one side of a puncture (Fig. 98); base of abdomen

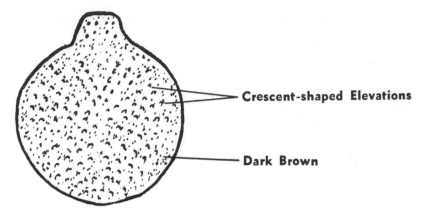

**Fig. 98**
**Crustulina guttata. Cephalothorax of Female.**

Crescent-shaped Elevations

Dark Brown

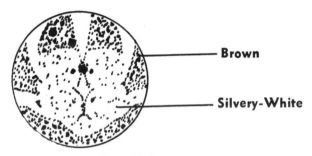

Brown

Silvery-White

**Fig. 98A**
**Crustulina guttata.**

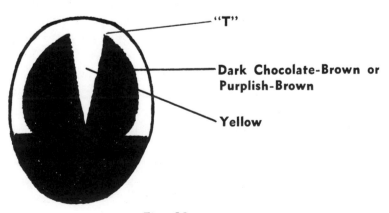

"T"

Dark Chocolate-Brown or
Purplish-Brown

Yellow

**Fig. 99**
**Steatoda borealis.**

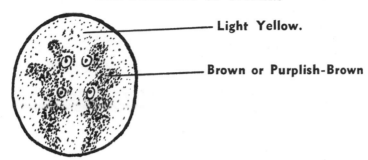

Light Yellow.

Brown or Purplish-Brown

Fig. 100
Teutana triangulosa.

with a horny ring around the insertion of the pedicel; sternum truncate behind; male with stridulating organs. Cephalothorax dark brown; abdomen spherical and sometimes bright yellow or orange without markings on back but more often it is partly brown with two or three pairs of silvery white spots (Fig. 98A); legs lighter than cephalothorax and more yellow.

Common under stones in fields and pastures.

Throughout the United States.

*Steatoda borealis.* About ⅕ inch long. Anterior median eyes much larger than anterior laterals; sternum pointed behind; male with stridulating organs. Cephalothorax orange-brown covered with short stiff hairs; abdomen dark chocolate brown or purplish brown with a yellow median line on the anterior half which joins a light line encircling the anterior half to form a "T"; legs brown with faint darker rings and thickly covered with hairs (Fig. 99).

Found in low herbage, beneath bark and stones, on bridges, and in buildings.

Web an irregular more or less flat sheet supported and held down by threads.

Widely distributed throughout the northern half of the United States.

*Teutana triangulosa.* Female ⅕ to ¼ inch long; male ⅛ inch. Posterior median eyes as large as anterior medians; male with stridulating organs. Cephalothorax orange-brown; abdomen light yellow with two irregular brown or purplish-brown stripes partly broken into spots and sometimes connected together; legs light yellow with slightly darker rings at the ends of the segments (Fig. 100).

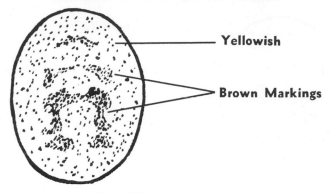

**Fig. 101**
**Lithyphantes corollatus.**

Lives under stones, culverts and in houses around window frames and similar places.

Web an imperfect sheet with a number of vertical guy-lines extending down from it.

Egg sac white and attached to the web.

New England south to Alabama and west to Colorado.

*Lithyphantes corollatus.* Female from ⅕ to ¼ inch long. Lateral eyes of each side narrowly but distinctly separate; male with stridulating organs. Cephalothorax dark brown; abdomen yellowish above with four or five more or less connected transverse brown bands and dark below with three narrow yellow lines connected behind; legs light brown with dark rings at the ends of the segments (Fig. 101).

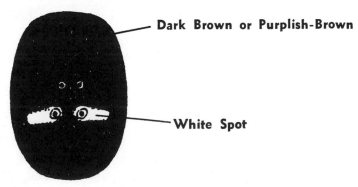

**Fig. 102**
**Asagena americana.**

Found under stones.

Widely distributed in the North.

*Lithyphantes fulvus.* Female from ⅕ to ¼ inch long. Cephalothorax reddish; abdomen brownish-yellow with two white spots on each side.

A southern species occurring from Florida to Texas and northward.

*Asagena americana.* Female about ⅙ inch long; male somewhat smaller. Cephalothorax dark reddish-brown (Fig. 102); abdomen oval and dark brown or dark purplish-brown with two white spots across the middle; legs yellow-brown. Male with stridulating organs (Fig. 102A).

Lives in its web under stones and logs and debris.

The Atlantic Coast from Maine to Florida and west to Washington.

*Enoplognatha marmorata.* Female about ¼ inch long; male somewhat smaller. Lateral eyes of each side contiguous; male with stridulating organs. Cephalothorax yellowish-brown with a few hairs; abdomen white to gray with usually an oblong dark spot covering the greater part of the upper surface, the middle being lighter with a central dark spot, though in some individuals the dark markings are broken up into four pairs of black spots partly connected with a middle line (Fig. 103); legs yellowish and covered with fine hairs.

This spider is found under stones, rock ledges, sometimes under leaves, and in bushes.

Maine south to Georgia and west to the Mississippi.

*Robertus (Ctenium) riparius.* Female about ⅙ inch long; male about the same or slightly smaller. Fourth pair of legs a little longer than first pair; sternum narrowly rounded behind; lateral eyes of each side

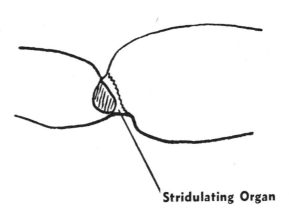

**Stridulating Organ**

**Fig. 102A**
**Asagena americana.**

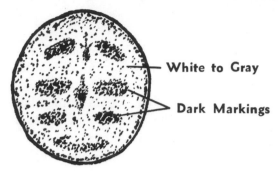

White to Gray

Dark Markings

Fig. 103
Enoplognatha marmorata.

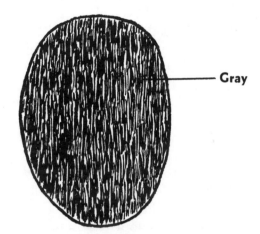

Gray

Fig. 104
Robertus riparius.

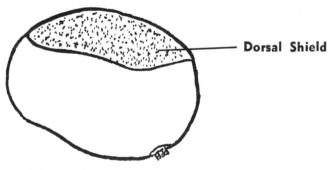

Dorsal Shield

Fig. 105
Ancylorrhanis hirsutum. Abdomen of Male.

contiguous. Cephalothorax yellowish-brown, smooth, shining; abdomen gray and covered with dark gray hairs (Fig. 104).

Occurs under leaves, stones, and boards on the ground.

Maine south to North Carolina and west to Wyoming.

*Ancylorrhanis hirsutum.* Female about $\frac{1}{16}$ inch long; male the same length. Sternum broadly truncate; abdomen large and globular; in the male upper surface of abdomen with a shield (Fig. 105); in the female a small plate over the pedicel; femora of front legs of male armed with stiff bristles. Cephalothorax brown with indistinct gray markings; abdomen whitish to pale gray; legs like cephalothorax (Fig. 105A).

Beneath woodland litter.

Maine south to North Carolina and west to Iowa and Missouri.

## THE SHEET-WEB WEAVERS

*Family Linyphiidae*

This family contains more species than any of our other families but as most of them are so small, even minute, and as they live hidden away in dark places under the natural debris on the ground, in shady woods, among the lower branches of plants and beneath the leaves of trees, and in caves, animal burrows and cellars, they are not often seen. Some, however, are of larger size and build more or less conspicuous webs which, though of various forms, usually

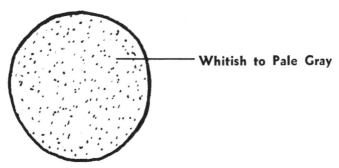

**Fig. 105A**
**Ancylorrhanis hirsutum. Abdomen of Female.**

contain one or more sheets of silk; hence they are generally called the sheet-web weavers.

The linyphiids, as they are also sometimes known, are three-clawed, eight-eyed spiders with more elongated bodies than the comb-footed spiders with which they were once classed. The chelicerae are large, strong, and well-toothed and in some species are provided with a row of striae that serves as a stridulating area, and the legs are set with long spines. These spiders are divided into two groups which are considered by many araneologists as separate families but they are here included in the same family. The two groups are the Erigonids and the Linyphiids.

## THE ERIGONIDS

*Subfamily Erigoninae*

The erigonids, which have been placed in the family Micryphantidae by some araneologists, are very small spiders not often seen unless they are looked for. They usually live on or near the ground, among dead leaves and in grass and moss where some of them build delicate webs which are practically invisible unless covered with dew. In autumn many of them become aeronautic, in fact, at this time of the year they probably form the greater part or at least a great part of ballooning spiders. Their small size, of course, is to their advantage when sailing through the air.

*Ceraticelus fissiceps.* This little spider is among the smallest species, measuring $\frac{1}{16}$ inch long. Cephalothorax and abdomen short and round, orange in color, abdomen with a round thickened spot on back more deeply colored; head black around the eyes with a transverse furrow back of the anterior median eyes which is shallow in the female and deep in the male (Fig. 106). Common on low bushes in summer and under leaves in winter.

*Ceraticelus laetabilis.* About the same size as *fissiceps.* Cephalothorax dark brown; in the male the upper surface is covered with a dark orange-brown shield, in the female the shield is usually reduced to four spots and the abdomen dark gray; legs dark orange. In dead leaves and moss, frequently under stones.

*Gnathonagrus unicorn.* About the same size as the two preceding species. Cephalothorax yellowish, abdomen olive-gray; legs yellowish.

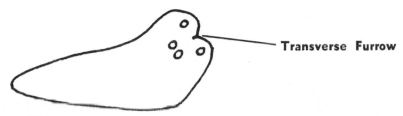

**Transverse Furrow**

**Fig. 106**
**Ceraticelsus fissiceps. Cephalothorax Showing Transverse Furrow.**


Male with a long horn, clothed with stiff hairs at the end, projecting from the middle of the clypeus (Fig. 107).

*Cornicularia directa.* Both male and female about $\frac{1}{12}$ inch long. Cephalothorax long narrowing gradually toward the head and brown; abdomen silver-gray. Male with a horn, covered on the upper side with stiff hairs, projecting forward from the eye space and a smaller horn below it (Fig. 108). Found under leaves.

*OEdothorax montiferus.* Both male and female about $\frac{1}{12}$ inch long. Hump on the cephalothorax of male which is as large as the rest of the cephalothorax (Fig. 108A). Hump contains cavities which open by holes on either side, the holes being connected by a deep crease which extends around the front of the hump. Anterior medians near together in the middle of the head in front of the hump, the other eyes are in two groups at the extreme corners of the head. Cephalothorax dark yellowish-brown; abdomen dark gray; legs orange-brown.

*Eperigone maculata.* About $\frac{1}{16}$ inch long. Cephalothorax yellowish-

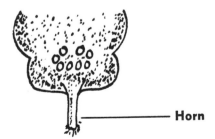

**Horn**

**Fig. 107**
**Gnathonagrus unicorn. Head of Male Showing Horn.**

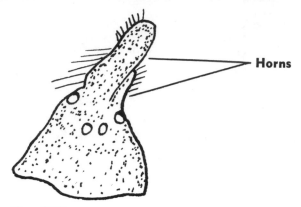

Horns

**Fig. 108**
**Cornicularia directa. Head of Male Showing Horns.**

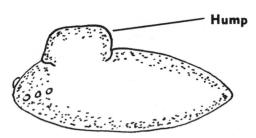

Hump

**Fig. 108A**
**Oedothorax montiferous. Cephalothorax of Male Showing Hump.**

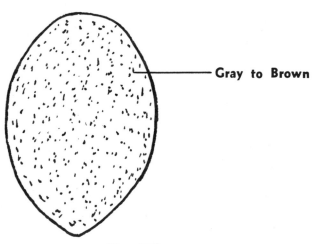

Gray to Brown

**Fig. 109**
**Microneta viara.**

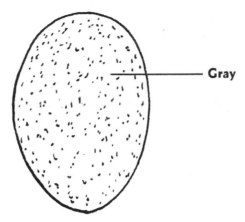

Gray

**Fig. 110**
**Bathyphantes concolor.**

brown; abdomen gray with several pairs of indistinct yellowish markings; legs dull yellow. This species is probably the most common of the erigonids.

*Erigone autumnalis.* This is a tiny spider, measuring only $\frac{1}{20}$ inch long, but may easily be recognized by its light color and bright yellow head.

*Ceratinopsis interpres.* Both male and female about $\frac{1}{10}$ inch long. Bright orange with a little black around the eyes and spinnerets. On low bushes.

## THE LINYPHIIDS

*Subfamily Linyphiinae*

These are the larger and better known of the sheet-web weavers some of which are very common and build rather elaborate webs.

*Microneta viaria.* Both male and female about $\frac{1}{6}$ inch long. Posterior eyes close together, laterals on slight tubercles; body rather slender; legs long and slender. Cephalothorax yellowish-brown; abdomen gray or brown; legs yellow (Fig. 109).

Found under leaves in woods and in deep ravines.

New England west to the Rockies.

*Bathyphantes concolor.* Male and female about $\frac{1}{12}$ inch long. Sternum heart-shaped; legs long, tibiae with lateral spines; abdomen slightly

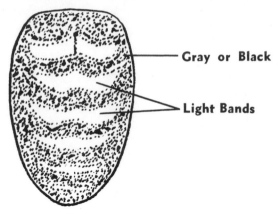

**Fig. 111**
**Bathyphantes nigrinus.**

pointed toward the spinnarets. Cephalothorax yellowish-brown; abdomen gray; legs yellow (Fig. 110).

Found under leaves.

A common species in the North.

*Bathyphantes nigrinus.* Male and female about $\frac{1}{10}$ inch long. Sternum and legs as in *concolor*; abdomen high in front and a little pointed behind. Cephalothorax light yellowish-brown; abdomen dark gray or black with five or six transverse light bands (Fig. 111).

Found under leaves.

Maine south to North Carolina and west to Illinois.

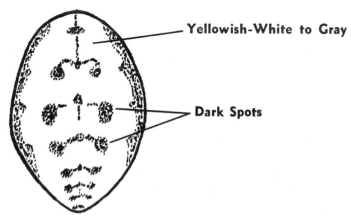

**Fig. 112**
**Lephthyphantes nebulosus.**

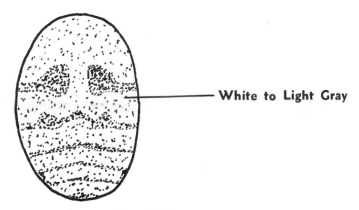

**Fig. 112A**
**Lephthyphantes zebra.**

*Lephthyphantes nebulosus.* Female ⅙ inch long; male somewhat smaller. Metatarsi with one or more spines. Cephalothorax brownish-yellow or orange with a dark marginal line and a dark middle stripe which forks in front toward the eyes; abdomen yellowish-white to gray with six or seven pairs of irregular dark spots more or less connected with a dark median line; legs with dark rings on the ends and middle of the femora and tibia (Fig. 112).

This spider lives in damp and shady places and is sometimes found

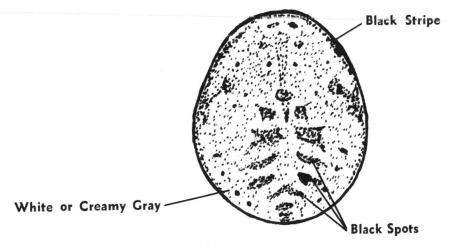

**Fig. 113**
**Drapetisca alterenda.**

in cellars. The snare is a large, flat sheet-web built close to the ground beneath stones and boards.

Maine south to Georgia and west to the Pacific.

*Lephthyphantes zebra.* Female about ⅛ inch long; male somewhat smaller. Cephalothorax yellow, darker along the margin; abdomen white to light gray with scattered silvery spots and several transverse dark bands which are sometimes indistinct (Fig. 112A).

The web is built among the curled up dead leaves on the woodland floor.

New England south to North Carolina and west to the Pacific.

*Drapetisca alteranda.* Female ⅛ inch long; male somewhat smaller. Chelicerae with three or four conspicuous spines on front surface. Cephalothorax white or creamy gray with a dark margin on each side and a black band in the middle with a series of more or less distinct black spots between it and the margin; abdomen broadly oval, widest just beyond the middle, white or creamy gray, mottled with gray, with a black stripe on each side and several pairs of black spots in the middle, connected with a median line; legs white with a gray ring at the end and middle of each segment (Fig. 113).

This spider is found under leaves on the ground but is more commonly seen either sitting or walking on tree trunks, especially aspens, birches and beeches which it matches in color and thus is difficult to see. It does not spin a web.

In the northern part of the United States, from Maine to Wisconsin.

*Linyphia clathrata.* Female about ⅛ inch long; male about the same

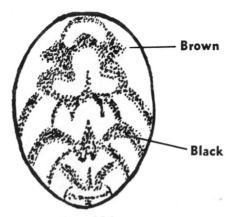

**Fig. 114**
**Linyphia clathrata.**

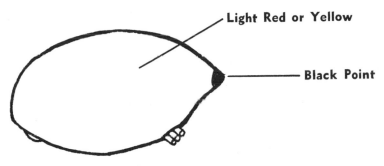

Light Red or Yellow

Black Point

Fig. 115
Linyphia coccinea.

or slightly smaller. Sternum longer than wide; posterior eyes widely separated. Cephalothorax brown or yellowish-brown; abdomen pale brown with a pattern of black chevrons (Fig. 114). Male darker with abdomen sometimes all black with a white spot on each side.

In ground litter and stones of wooded areas; also in salt marshes. Web a flat sheet built near the ground.

Maine south to North Carolina and west to the Pacific Coast.

*Linyphia (Florinda) coccinea.* Female ⅙ inch long; male slightly smaller. Cephalothorax orange to red with black in the region of the eyes; abdomen light red or yellow; legs light orange; abdomen somewhat flattened on top and extended back in a blunt point over the spinnerets (Fig. 115). Male much like female except for a more slender abdomen and longer legs.

The spider lives in grass and on low plants where it builds a web that is somewhat concave.

This is a common species in the South; from Maryland south to Florida and Texas and west to Illinois.

*Linyphia variabilis.* Female about ⅛ inch long; male slightly smaller. Cephalothorax yellowish-brown; abdomen, which is comparatively high and ending in a more or less pronounced rounded projection located rather high above the spinnerets, reddish or yellowish above with a few silvery spots and a dark spot on the rounded tip (Fig. 115A).

Northeastern States.

*Linyphia (Frontinella) communis. The Bowl and Doily Spider.* Female about ⅙ inch long; male slightly smaller. Cephalothorax evenly brown or uniformly light brownish-yellow; abdomen about as high

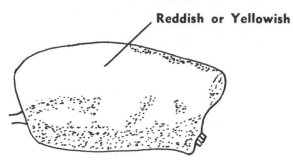

**Fig. 115A**
**Linyphia variabilis.**

above spinnerets as in front, whitish, with a middle stripe that extends the entire length of the upper surface (Fig. 116).

This spider lives usually in low bushes where it spins its web sometimes quite near the ground, at other times several feet above the surface. The web is a fingerbowl-like cup beneath which is stretched a nearly horizontal sheet.

Maine south to Florida and west to Arizona and the Dakotas.

*Linyphia (Helophora) insignis.* Female about ⅛ inch long; male slightly smaller. Cephalothorax yellow or light orange-yellow; abdomen dark gray or white and is either unmarked or with gray stripes or spots on the sides and two or three pairs of gray marks across the posterior half; legs light yellow (Fig. 117).

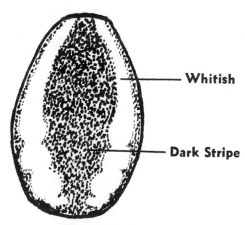

**Fig. 116**
**Linyphia communis.**

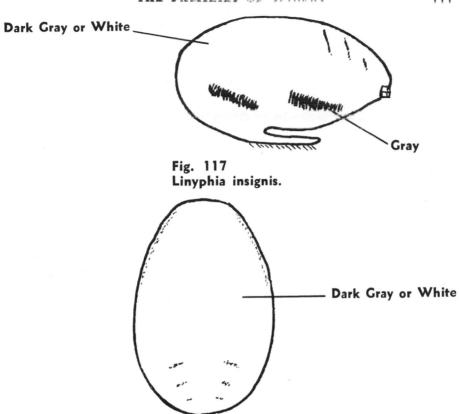

**Dark Gray or White**

**Gray**

**Fig. 117**
**Linyphia insignis.**

**Dark Gray or White**

This spider lives in webs built near the ground in grass and low bushes.

New England west to Utah.

*Linyphia (Stemoynphantes) lineata.* Female about ¼ inch long; male about ⅕ inch. General color light yellowish-gray, the cephalothorax with a broad middle and narrow marginal black stripes and the abdomen with three rows of black spots which makes it easy to distinguish from other species of *Linyphia;* legs with dark rings at the end and middle of the segments (Fig. 118).

Found under stones and logs in the woods.

Maine south to Virginia and west to the Pacific Coast.

*Linyphia marginata. The Filmy Dome Spider.* Both male and female about ⅙ inch long. Cephalothorax two-thirds as wide as long, dark brown in the middle with lateral margins white; abdomen yellowish-

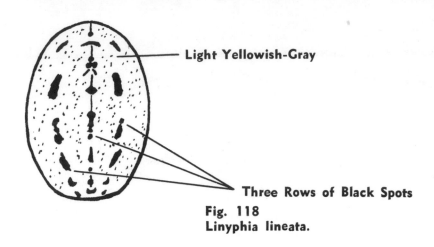

Light Yellowish-Gray

Three Rows of Black Spots

Fig. 118
Linyphia lineata.

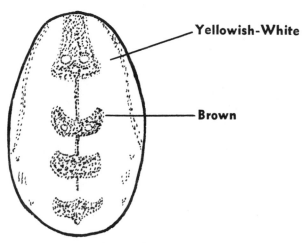

Yellowish-White

Brown

Fig. 119
Linyphia marginata

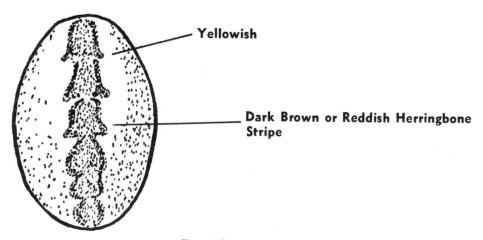

Yellowish

Dark Brown or Reddish Herringbone
Stripe

Fig. 120
Linyphia phrygiana.

white with several brown stripes on the sides and a dark stripe in the middle consisting usually of three parts united by a narrow line and with a dark spot behind it; legs light yellow without markings (Fig. 119).

This spider is found on herbs and low bushes in wooded areas and also about rock piles and stone walls. Web in the form of a dome four or five inches in diameter, suspended between rocks or plants, and so transparent that it easily escapes notice unless the sun shines on it.

A common species from Maine south to Florida and west to California.

*Linyphia (Pityohyphantes) phrygiana. The Hammock Spider.* Female about ⅕ inch long; male somewhat smaller. Cephalothorax light yellow or white with thin black lines at the margins and a black line in the middle forked at the front end; abdomen yellowish with a dark brown or reddish herring-bone stripe in the middle; legs light yellow with a dark ring at the end of each segment and at the middle of each tibia and metatarsus (Fig. 120).

This is a common species living both in the woods and around houses. Web a large flat sheet, sometimes over a foot across, and built chiefly on herbaceous plants but also on shrubs, the lower branches of trees, fences, and even in garages and other outbuildings.

Maine south to North Carolina and west to the Pacific.

*Linyphia pusilla. The Platform Spider.* Female about ⅙ inch long; male slightly smaller. Cephalothorax dark brown or dark orange-brown; abdomen dark brown, sometimes almost black, with several

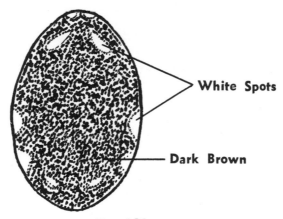

White Spots

Dark Brown

**Fig. 121**
**Linyphia pusilla**

white spots, usually two across the anterior and with several on the sides which often form a complete white margin; in some individuals the upper surface is brown with a series of transverse dark bands; legs same color as cephalothorax but a lighter shade (Fig. 121).

The spider lives in fields and meadows where it spins its web between blades of grass. It is a horizontal platform, from three to six inches in diameter and usually from two to six inches above the ground, with a labyrinth of delicate threads above it. As a rule the spider hangs below the center of the platform but sometimes is found in the labyrinth; it is very shy and drops to the ground at any disturbance.

Maine south to Virginia and west to the Pacific.

*Tapinopa bilineata.* Female about ⅙ inch long. Anterior median eyes larger than posterior medians which are closer to the posterior laterals than each other. Cephalothorax dark brown or gray on the sides with a median light line widest in front and narrowing to a point behind; abdomen pale grayish-brown, blotched with white, with two rows of four or five spots and a few chevrons at the tip (Fig. 122).

Lives in grass or leaves close to the ground.

Maine south to Georgia and west to Wisconsin.

## THE ORB-WEAVERS

*Family (Argiopidae) Araneidae*

The Araneidae includes the spiders that spin the webs that attract

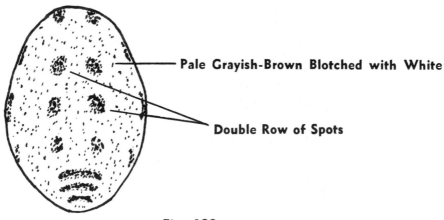

Fig. 122
Tapinopa bilineata.

our attention and excite our admiration as we roam the countryside and follow the woodland trail in late summer. The spiders have three claws, eight eyes that are similar in most of the species, and tarsi that are more or less clothed with hairs. They are sedentary in habits and remain for the most part on their webs where they await a prospective insect victim.

The Araneidae, formerly known as the Argiopidae, consists of a number of sub-families, a few of which have been established as separate families by some araneologists. We are including in the family

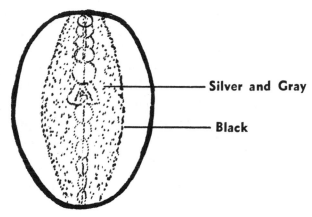

**Fig. 123**
**Pachygnatha tristriata.**

The Tetragnathids, The Metids, The Silk Spiders, The Garden Spiders, The Typical Orb Weavers and The Spiny-bellied Spiders and are treating The Ray-spiders, formerly included, as a separate family.

## THE TETRAGNATHIDS

*Subfamily Tetragnathinae*

The tetragnathids are for the most part greatly elongated spiders with very long thin legs and chelicerae of great size, especially in the males; hence they are often referred to as the big-jawed spiders. Most of them live in grassy places and are particularly common on the borders of swamps and on the banks of streams. Their webs are usually inclined or vertical and framed in grass or shrubs but sometimes they are extended horizontally over water. They are rather delicate in composition and are best fitted for entrapping midges, crane-flies, and other small insects that are not strong flyers. The egg sacs, which are attached to various objects, have a somewhat characteristic appearance because they have projecting tufts of silk that in many instances are of a different color than the rest of the sac.

*Pachygnatha tristriata.* Female about ¼ inch long; male about the same. Cephalothorax yellowish-brown, somewhat darker along the sides; abdomen with a folium of silver and gray bordered with black (Fig. 123).

This spider is found on the ground in deep grass, under stones, wood, or leaves usually in damp places, especially cattail swamps. Does not spin a web but wanders in search of small insect prey.

Maine south to Georgia and west to Nebraska and Texas.

*Note:* Two other species of Pachygnatha occur throughout the East. They are *P. autumnalis* and *P. brevis* both of which are similar to *tristriata* except that they have a folium with scalloped edges and in *autumnalis* the posterior median eyes are much larger than the others whereas in *brevis* they are not larger than the anterior medians.

*Glenognatha foxi.* Female about ⅛ inch long; male about the same. Rather globose in outline and colored pink and silver.

Found in meadows and grassy places. The orb web, a delicate affair, three or four inches across, is usually built horizontally in grasses and weeds about two inches above the ground.

Occurs all over the South.

*Tetragnatha elongata.* Female about ½ inch long; male somewhat smaller. Lateral eyes of each side closer together than the medians are; chelicerae of male longer than the cephalothorax and almost as long in the females; abdomen broad near the base, tapering toward the posterior end. General color reddish brown, sometimes yellow or gray with gray markings on the cephalothorax and brownish markings on the abdomen (Fig. 124).

Prefers damp situations; web often found over running water. Egg sacs attached to twigs and sparsely covered with threads of beadlike greenish silk.

Throughout the United States.

*Tetragnatha laboriosa.* Female about ⅓ inch long; male a little smaller. Lateral eyes of each side as far apart as the medians; abdomen of female less than three times as long as cephalothorax; chelicerae short and almost vertical, one-half to two-thirds length of cephalo-

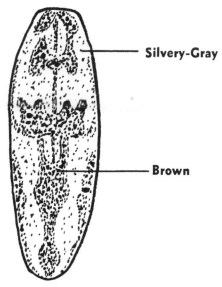

**Fig. 124**
**Tetragnatha elongata.**

thorax in males and shorter in females. General color light yellow
with abdomen silvery white; some indistinct gray markings along
the middle (Fig. 125).

Common in meadows; web made between grass stems.

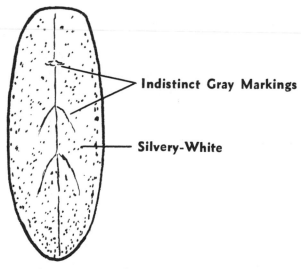

**Fig. 125**
**Tetragnatha laboriosa.**

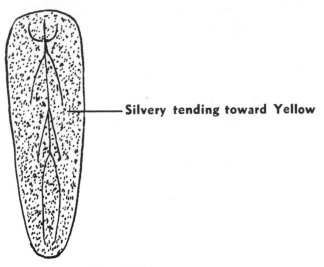

Silvery tending toward Yellow

**Fig. 126**
**Tetragnatha straminea.**

Throughout the United States.
*Tetragnatha straminea.* Female ¼ to ⅜ inch long; male somewhat smaller. Lateral eyes of each side farther apart than the medians; abdomen of female usually three times as long as cephalothorax. Cephalothorax light yellow; abdomen silvery white. In appearance similar to *laboriosa* (Fig. 126).

Maine south to Florida and west to Minnesota and Texas.
*Tetragnatha extensa.* Female from ¼ to ⅜ inch long; male slightly smaller. Lateral eyes of each side closer together than are the medians; chelicerae of both male and female shorter than cephalothorax, in the female only a little more than half as long as the cephalothorax. General color dull yellowish-brown or gray with a middle dark stripe on the abdomen bordered on each side with a silvery stripe (Fig. 127).

Throughout the United States.

## THE METIDS

*Subfamily Metinae*

The metids are closely related to the tetragnathids but are somewhat more diversified in their appearance. Some live in caves and

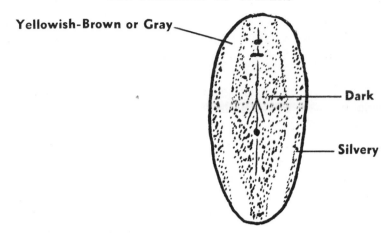

Yellowish-Brown or Gray

Dark

Silvery

**Fig. 127**
**Tetragnatha extensa.**

other dark places; others are found on bushes and trees and among these are some of our most brilliantly colored spiders.

*Allepeira conferta (Hentzia basilica). The Basilica Spider.* Female from ¼ to nearly ⅓ inch long; male somewhat smaller. Cephalothorax oval, yellow or olive, with a median black line and a wider one on each margin; abdomen cylindrical with a hump on each side near the base, yellow or olive-green with a black and yellow folium outlined in white (Fig. 127A).

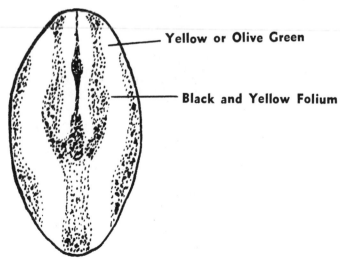

Yellow or Olive Green

Black and Yellow Folium

**Fig. 127A**
**Allepeira conferta.**

Found on bushes in well-shaded places. Web an orb pulled into a dome with a nearby labyrinth.

Egg sacs attached to each other in strings and suspended in the web (Fig. 127B).

A southern species, occurring from the District of Columbia south to Florida and west to Colorado.

*Meta menardii.* Female ½ inch or more long; male a third shorter. Lateral eyes of each side near together; cephalothorax large and broad; abdomen longer than wide, high in front and somewhat tapering toward the posterior end; legs long, the front pair twice the length of the body; chelicerae long, thickened in front near the base; dorsal groove very deep. Cephalothorax yellowish to brown with a median and lateral stripes; abdomen dark brown to purple with a middle stripe, a little middle spot in front and several middle spots and pairs of spots diminishing backward; legs with gray rings at the middle and ends of the segments (Fig. 128).

Found in caves, deserted mines, deep recesses of cliffs, and similar cool and shady places. Web usually inclined but may be vertical or horizontal depending on the shape of the rocks where it is made.

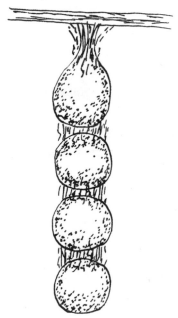

**Fig. 127B**
**Egg Sacs of Allepeira conferta.**

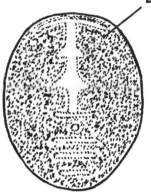

Dark Brown to Purple

Fig. 128
Meta menardii.

Fig. 129
Egg Sac of Meta menardii.

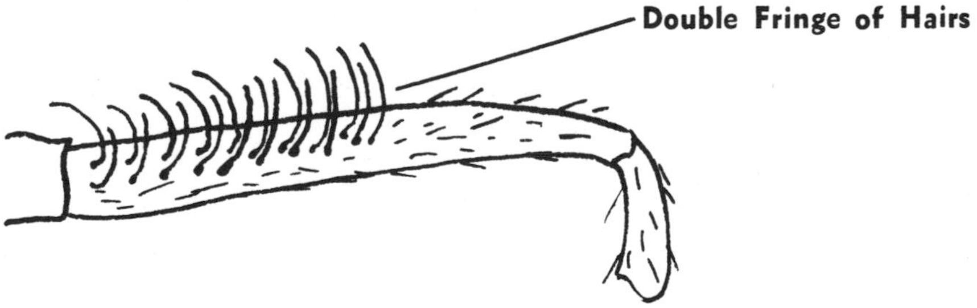

Double Fringe of Hairs

Fig. 130
Leucauge venusta.
Femur of Hind Leg, Showing Double Fringe of Hairs.

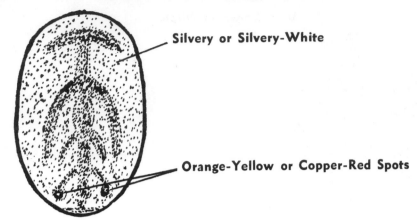

Silvery or Silvery-White

Orange-Yellow or Copper-Red Spots

**Fig. 131**
**Leucauge venusta.**

Egg sac large, snowy-white, and translucent (Fig. 129).

Maine south to Virginia and west to the Mississippi.

*Leucauge venusta. The Beautiful Leucauge.* Female from ⅕ to ¼ inch long; male about half as long. Femora of hind legs with a double fringe of hairs (Fig. 130); epigastric furrow nearly straight; abdomen elliptical, twice as long as wide; legs long and slender, especially the first two pairs. Cephalothorax yellowish or yellowish-green with a dark or green stripe on each side; abdomen silvery or silvery-white with a dark line in the middle from which extend four pairs of more or less distinct bars and sometimes with two bright orange-yellow or copper-red spots above near the posterior end and a red spot in the middle of the lower surface (Fig. 131).

This is one of the most beautiful of all our spiders. It lives in the open well-lighted situations and builds its web, which may be either horizontal or inclined and often more than a foot across, on shrubs and trees.

Maine south to Florida and west to the Mississippi River.

*Nesticus pallidus.* Female ⅐ inch long; male slightly smaller. Lateral eyes on each side close together, median eyes of first row smaller than the others; tarsi with serrated bristles. Cephalothorax pale orange-brown; abdomen yellowish-white with brown hairs; legs same color as cephalothorax.

Lives under stones or boards on the ground, in burrows and cave entrances, and in dark caves.

Throughout the United States.

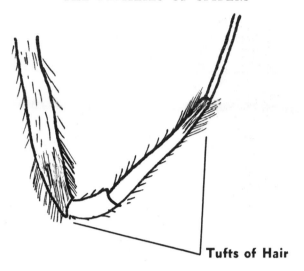

**Tufts of Hair**

**Fig. 132**
**Nephila clavipes. Leg Showing Tufts of Hairs on Femur and Tibia.**

## THE SILK SPIDERS

*Subfamily Nephilinae*

The spiders of this subfamily are essentially tropical species and are the largest of all the orb weavers, often more than two inches

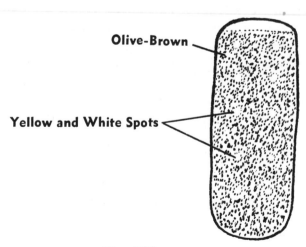

**Olive-Brown**

**Yellow and White Spots**

**Fig. 133**
**Nephila clavipes.**

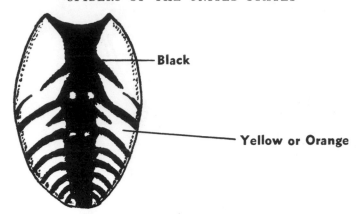

**Fig. 134**
**Miranda aurantia.**

long and with legs that sometimes span eight inches. They are remarkable for the amount and the strength of the silk they spin and are rightly known as the silk spiders. Their great round webs of golden silk, which are sometimes more than three feet in diameter, are often made high in trees or across trails in the forest. We have only one species.

*Nephila clavipes. The Golden-silk Spider.* Female from ⅞ to 1¹⁄₁₀ inch long; male considerably smaller. Eyes quite small and nearly all the same size; cephalothorax longer than wide; abdomen two and one-half to three times as long as broad with nearly parallel sides; legs long and, except for third pair, with conspicuous tufts of hair on femora and tibia (Fig. 132). Cephalothorax dark brown; abdomen olive-brown with pairs of yellow and white spots and a light line across anterior end (Fig. 133).

Found in shady places. Web usually a large orb, slightly inclined, in trees, in shaded woods; viscid spiral of a yellowish color rather than white.

A southern species found from Florida west to California.


## THE GARDEN SPIDERS

*Subfamily Argiopinae*

To this subfamily belong the handsome orb weavers whose bright colors and conspicuous webs make them familiar creatures on the summer landscape. These spiders, which are commonly known as the garden spiders, differ from other spiders of the family in having the posterior row of eyes strongly procurved. Their webs are ordinarily somewhat inclined but they may at times be vertical and are provided with a sheet hub. A barrier web may frequently be associated with them. Sometimes a stabilimentum is vaguely indicated but usually it is a conspicuous feature of the web, indeed, it might be said to be the signature of this group of spiders.

*Miranda (Argiope) aurantia. The Orange Garden Spider.* Female an inch or more long; male about one-fourth as long. Cephalothorax nearly as wide as long and covered with silvery white hairs; abdomen oval, a little pointed behind, with a pair of humps at the base, a black stripe in the middle narrowed between the humps and widened in the middle where it includes two pairs of yellow or orange spots, two bright yellow or orange bands or rows of spots along sides; front legs entirely black, others black with reddish or yellow femora (Fig. 134). Male similarly colored but with markings less distinct.

Lives in fields, meadows, marshy places and gardens. Web sometimes built on shrubs but more frequently upon grass and herbaceous growth and sometimes as much as two feet in diameter.

Egg sac, pear-shaped, about the size of a hickory nut (Fig. 20), with a brownish, tough papery cover and attached to the top of some herbaceous plant or fastened among the branches of a shrub by many strands of silk.

Throughout the United States.

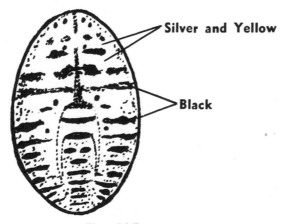

**Silver and Yellow**

**Black**

**Fig. 135**
**Argiope trifasciata.**

*Argiope (Metargiope) trifasciata. The Banded Garden Spider.* Female from ⅗ to ⅘ inch long; male about ⅕ inch. The ground color is white or light yellow, the cephalothorax with silvery hairs, and the abdomen with many thin silver and yellow transverse lines alternating with black, lacking the humps of *aurantia;* legs light yellow with black bands at the ends and middle of the segments (Fig. 135).

Found in essentially the same situations as *aurantia* but perhaps more often in drier locations. Web much the same as that of *aurantia.*

Egg sac cup-shaped with a flattened top, perhaps like that of a kettle drum, with a brown, tough, papery cover and fastened among the branches of a low shrub or between the leaves of a herbaceous plant (Fig. 23).

Throughout the United States.

*Argiope argentata. The Silver Garden Spider.* This is a tropical species whose range extends into the southern states, being locally abundant from Florida to California. It is about ¾ inch long, metallic silver and yellow, with the abdomen divided in the posterior half into rounded lobes.


## THE TYPICAL ORB-WEAVERS

*Subfamily Araneinae*

As most of the orb-weavers belong to this subfamily they are generally referred to as the typical orb-weavers. They are generally thick-set in appearance, with bulky abdomens and relatively short legs, though some are rather long and narrow. The web is circular in outline for the most part but details of construction vary with the different species.

*Glyptocranium cornigerum.* Female ½ inch long; male ⅒ inch. Cephalothorax with four large tubercles (Fig. 135A); abdomen nearly spherical. Cephalothorax red or reddish-brown and yellow with dark brown markings; abdomen yellow with dark or brownish markings on the anterior part.

This spider when resting on a leaf folds its legs and resembles bird-lime.

Southern states.

*Glyptocranium bisaccutum.* Female ⅓ to ⁴⁄₁₀ inch long; male ⅛ inch. Cephalothorax scalloped at the sides and covered with scattered conical points rises upward backward from the eyes (Fig. 135B) with

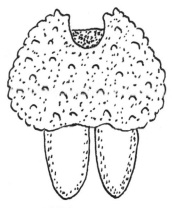

**Fig. 135A**
**Glyptocranium cornigerum.**
**Front View of Cephalothorax.**

**Fig. 135B**
**Side View of Glyptocranium bissacatum.**

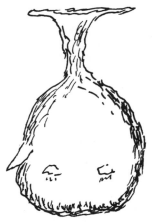

**Fig. 135C**
**Egg Sac of Glyptocranium bissacatum.**

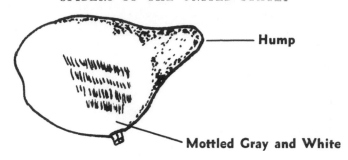

**Fig. 136**
**Cyclosa conica.**

two large horns at the highest part; abdomen wider in front than long and extends over the thorax as far as the two horns. Cephalothorax light brown; abdomen light brown with various irregular whitish markings on anterior part, yellowish-white on posterior part.

Egg sac dark brown (Fig. 135C).

Northern states.

*Cyclosa conica.* Female ¼ to ⅓ inch long; male much smaller. Both rows of eyes recurved, posterior medians almost together; caudal end of abdomen in female extended into a prominent hump, only a slight trace of it in the male; head and thorax separated by a deep cervical groove, at least in the female. Cephalothorax dark gray or black; abdomen mottled with gray and white; there are marked variations in color, some individuals being almost white while others are nearly black; in light individuals the markings on the abdomen are obscure

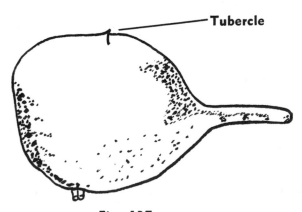

**Fig. 137**
**Cyclosa turbinata.**

but there is usually a distinct dark middle stripe; legs white with dark rings at the end of each segment and in the middle of each except the femora (Fig. 136).

This spider is common in open woodlands where the web, which is remarkable for its symmetry and for the fineness of its meshes, is built upon shrubs, usually with a short stabilimentum.

Throughout the United States.

*Cyclosa caroli.* A southern species, gray in color, ¼ to ⅓ inch long, with a very long and slender abdomen.

*Cyclosa bifurca.* The odd form of the abdomen makes this species easy

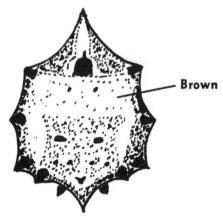

— Brown

**Fig. 137A**
**Marxia stellata.**

to recognize from other *Cyclosas*. It is long with two pairs of humps on the anterior half and bifurcate at the posterior end. Body green mottled with white; abdomen with a light wavy band on the sides and bordered with a black line above in back of the humps.

A southern species.

*Cyclosa turbinata.* This species of *Cyclosa* is also found throughout the United States but seems to be more common in the South than in the North. The female may readily be identified by the shape of the abdomen which is extended into a slender caudal projection; there is also a pair of median tubercles on the upper surface (Fig. 137).

*Marxia (Acanthepeira) stellata.* Female ¼ to ⅓ inch long; male much smaller. Anterior row of eyes strongly procurved, lateral eyes of each side under a conical tubercle; cephalothorax wide in front; abdomen

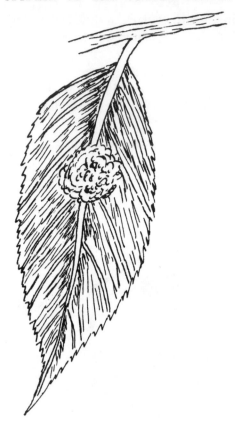

**Fig. 137B**
**Egg Sac of Marxia stellata.**

encircled with a series of tubercles with a sharp point in front that extends over the cephalothorax; legs short. Cephalothorax brown, lighter in the middle, darker at the sides, covered with short gray hairs; abdomen brown, lighter on the posterior two-thirds, with dark spots; legs with dark rings at the ends and middle of the segments (Fig. 137A).

This star-shaped spider lives in low bushes and among grass and herbaceous plants. Web from six to ten inches in diameter.

Egg sac a mass of loose brown silk and attached to a leaf (Fig. 137B).

Maine south to Florida and west to the Mississippi.

*Zilla atrica, Zilla x-notata, Zilla montana.* We have three species of *Zilla* in the East which resemble each other so closely that it is almost impossible to distinguish them except by examining the epigyna of the

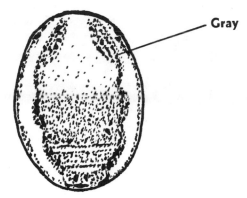

Gray

**Fig. 137C**
**Zilla atrica.**

females and the palpi of the males. They are of moderate size, the largest being about ⅜ inch long. The posterior median eyes are as close to the posterior laterals as to each other; head rounded in front; abdomen rather large, oval, and somewhat flattened; legs slender. The color of these spiders is gray, occasionally with a little yellow or pink, cephalothorax usually with a dark border at the sides and a middle dark line that widens towards the eyes, abdomen with a scalloped middle stripe crossed at the posterior end with two or three pairs of transverse spots (Figs. 137C).

*Atrica* and *x-notata* live on the outside of houses, *montana* in trees and rocks.

*Cercida prominens.* Female ⅕ inch long; male slightly smaller. Cuticula of the upper surface of the abdomen hard and glossy. Cephalothorax red; abdomen brownish above with a large reddish shield nearly covering the upper surface, with a suggestion of transverse black lines on posterior half; sternum black; legs yellowish with brown rings.

New England west to Illinois.

*Singa pratensis.* Female about ⅕ inch long; male slightly smaller. Posterior median eyes larger than anterior medians; abdomen as high behind its middle as at its base and elliptical in outline; legs short. Cephalothorax yellow; abdomen white or yellow with two broad longitudinal yellow-brown stripes darkening toward the posterior end; legs yellow (Fig. 138).

Lives among grass and other small plants in low open ground.
Throughout the United States.

*Singa variabilis.* Female ⅙ inch long; male ⅛ inch. Cephalothorax

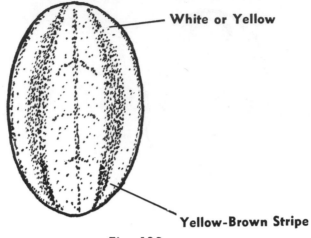

**Fig. 138**
**Singa pratensis.**

light orange, black around the eyes; abdomen usually entirely black but sometimes with bright yellow markings. Occasionally there is a wide middle stripe, with narrower stripes at the sides, or there may be only two lateral stripes with variations between these markings (Fig. 138A).

Throughout the United States.

*Singa truncata.* Female about ⅛ inch long; male about the same. Cephalothorax orange-brown with black around the eyes; abdomen

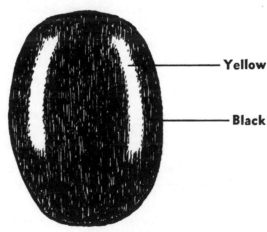

**Fig. 138A**
**Singa variabilis.**

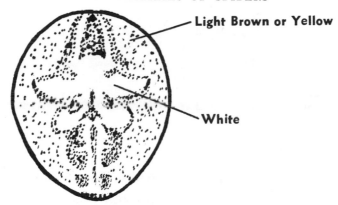

**Light Brown or Yellow**

**White**

**Fig. 139**
**Metepeira labyrinthea.**

orange with indistinct blackish markings across the posterior half.
Throughout the United States.

*Metepeira labyrinthea. The Labyrinth Spider.* Female from ¼ to ⅖ inch long. Metatarsus and tarsus of the first legs together longer than the tibia and patella; abdomen triangular-ovate. Cephalothorax dark brown, ocular area yellow; abdomen light brown or yellow on sides with a folium in which there is a central white band and two pairs of white spots extending laterally from it; legs dull yellow banded with brown; sternum brown or black with a central white or yellow band (Fig. 139).

Found in woodlands. Web a composite one, consisting of an incomplete vertical orb with an irregular net behind it.

Egg sac brown, lenticular; a string of egg sacs is attached to the irregular net.

Throughout the United States.

*Verrucosa arenata.* Female ⅜ inch long; male somewhat smaller. Head elevated above thorax; cervical groove deeply marked; abdomen triangular-ovate, flattened on top, with the posterior apex marked by a round tubercle and with the cuticula of the upper surface hard and glossy. Cephalothorax brown, the head much darker than the thoracic part. Abdomen (Fig. 140) almost completely covered with a large triangular spot which may be white, yellow, pink, or greenish varying in different individuals.

Found in woodlands and forests. Web fairly large with a coarse mesh and long guy lines.

Essentially a southern species found from New York south to

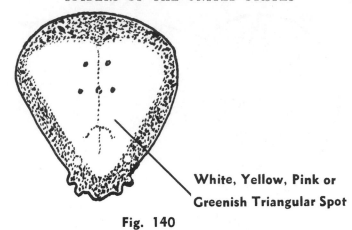

White, Yellow, Pink or
Greenish Triangular Spot

Fig. 140
Verrucosa arenata.

Florida and west to Nebraska and California.

*Note:* the genus *Aranea* is a very large one and the following species have been selected as being the most common and the ones most likely to be observed. In these spiders the cephalothorax is moderately arched, the median ocular area is wider in front than behind, the anterior and posterior median eyes are slightly unequal in size, and the lateral eyes of each side are contiguous or nearly so (Fig. 140A). Some of the araneas have a pair of prominent humps near the base of the abdomen and for this reason are generally known as the Angulate Araneas. The following five species belong to this group.

*Aranea angulata.* Female about ½ inch long; male about half the size. Cephalothorax dark brown with traces of darker lines in the middle and at the sides; abdomen with a yellow spot or group of yellow spots between or in front of the humps and with a distinct folium bordered by an undulating dark line; legs brown with darker rings at the ends of the segments and less distinct rings in the middle (Fig. 141). Pattern, however, a variable one.

Found in woods. Web often between trees high above the ground.

Throughout the East.

*Aranea nordmanni.* Female about ½ inch long; male about half as long. Cephalothorax light gray, darkest at the sides; abdomen with a folium on posterior half and with an indistinct dark area in front enclosing a long, white spot; legs with a dark ring at the ends and a lighter one in the middle of each segment. Pattern a variable one (Fig. 142).

Woodlands.

**Fig. 140A**
**Cephalothorax of Aranea Showing Arrangement of Eyes.**

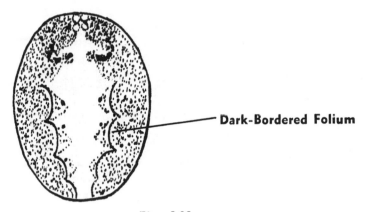

Dark-Bordered Folium

**Fig. 141**
**Aranea angulata.**

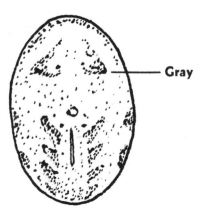

Gray

**Fig. 142**
**Aranea nordmanni.**

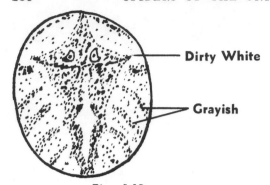

Fig. 143
Aranea cavatica.

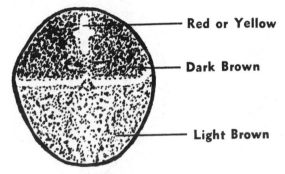

Fig. 144
Aranea corticaria.

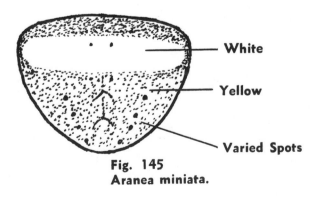

Fig. 145
Aranea miniata.

Maine south to North Carolina and west to the Pacific.

*Aranea cavatica.* Female about ¾ inch long; male smaller. General color a dirty white with grayish markings and with numerous whitish or grayish hairs which give it a somewhat grayish appearance; folium on abdomen similar to that of *angulata;* legs with gray rings at the ends and middle of the segments which may be quite indistinct in some individuals and very dark in others (Fig. 143).

Found in shady situations and about houses and barns.

Throughout the East.

*Aranea corticaria.* Female nearly ⅓ inch long; male smaller. Cephalothorax brown with sides lighter; abdomen yellowish-brown to dark brown with light markings on the anterior part that are often bright red or yellow, and with a narrow light line from the middle to each hump; legs with broken brown rings at the ends and the middle of each segment (Fig. 144).

New England and the North Middle Atlantic States.

*Aranea miniata.* Female less than ⅕ inch long; male about ⅛ inch. General color yellow or light yellow with paired dark or brown spots on the posterior half of the abdomen with a broad white transverse band between the humps (Fig. 145).

A southern species found from New England south to Florida and west to Oklahoma.

*Note:* The following five species of *araneas* do not have the humps of the angulate *araneas* and are generally called the Round-shouldered *Araneas.*

*Aranea gigas (marmoreus).* Female from ½ to ¾ inch long; male about half as long. Cephalothorax yellow with slightly darker lines in the middle and at the sides; abdomen bright yellow marked with brown, with a brown folium enclosing a central yellow band or series of yellow spots, the folium being outlined on each side by a wavy yellow stripe; sternum brown, light yellow in the middle; femur and patella of legs bright orange, darker towards the ends, other segments white with brown ends (Fig. 146).

Lives in wooded areas. Web one foot or more in diameter, nearly vertical, built in shrubs or among the low branches of trees with a retreat made in a curled leaf or in a bunch of leaves, the retreat being connected to the hub by one or more traplines.

Throughout the United States.

*Aranea trifolium. The Shamrock Spider.* Female from ½ to ¾ inch long; male about half as long. Cephalothorax white with three wide black stripes; upper surface of abdomen varies from dark purplish-brown to light gray or white, sometimes light yellow or even pale

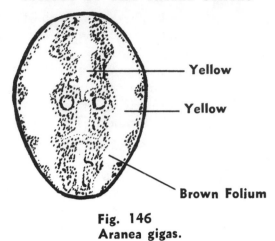

Fig. 146
Aranea gigas.

green with four white spots and a middle row of smaller spots with
several oblique rows still smaller; lower surface of abdomen dark
brown; legs conspicuously marked with dark rings (Fig. 147).

Found in open areas. Web made in bushes or in herbaceous growth
with a retreat in a folded leaf or a bunch of leaves above and at one
side of the orb, the retreat being connected to the center of the web
by a trapline.

Throughout the United States.

*Aranea thaddeus. The Lattice Spider.* Female about ¼ inch long; male
somewhat smaller. Cephalothorax varies from yellow to orange-yellow
to yellowish-brown; abdomen large and round (Fig. 148), white or

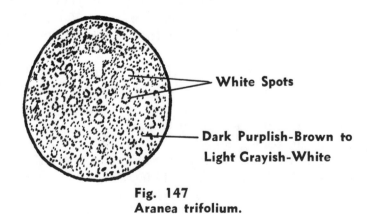

Fig. 147
Aranea trifolium.

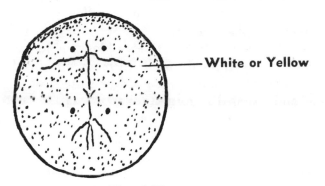

Fig. 148
Aranea thaddeus.

White or Yellow

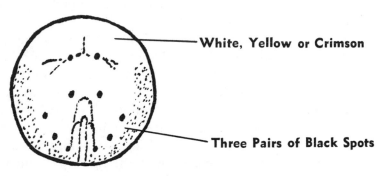

White, Yellow or Crimson

Three Pairs of Black Spots

Fig. 149
Aranea displicata.

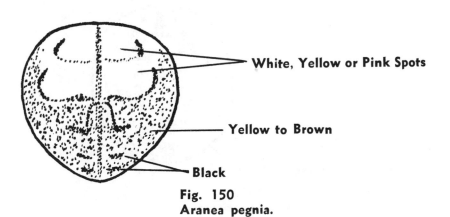

White, Yellow or Pink Spots

Yellow to Brown

Black

Fig. 150
Aranea pegnia.

yellow on the upper surface, brown on the lower with a yellow spot in the middle; legs same color as cephalothorax.

Found usually in dense foliage. Web sometimes oblong in form, at other times circular; retreat a cylindrical tube with many openings which make it look like lattice-work built on the lower surface of a leaf which has been bent and fastened to form a tent.

Throughout the eastern half of the United States.

*Aranea (Araniella) displicata.* Female about ¼ inch or less long; male about the same size. Cephalothorax yellow to brown or brownish-yellow without markings; abdomen oval, white, yellow, or crimson with three pairs of black spots on the posterior half (Fig. 149); legs same color as cephalothorax. Male with cephalothorax and legs darker brown and black spots on abdomen larger.

Lives in tall grass and bushes. Web a small one made among the leaves, sometimes in the space made by the bending of a single leaf.

Throughout the United States.

*Aranea (Neosconella) pegnia.* Female about ¼ inch long; male a third smaller. Cephalothorax yellow with a very narrow dark line extending from the eyes to the dorsal groove and indistinct dark marks on the sides of the head; abdomen globose being nearly as wide as long, yellow to brown with two pairs of large white, yellow or pink spots or bars on the anterior half and three or four pairs of black spots on the posterior half; first and second legs with slightly darker rings at the end and middle of each segment, the third and fourth at the ends of the segments only (Fig. 150). Male marked like the female, though the abdomen is more elongate than that of the female.

In bushes but also about buildings. Web a composite one, con-

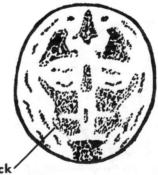

**Brown, Tending to Black**

**Fig. 151**
**Aranea sericata.**

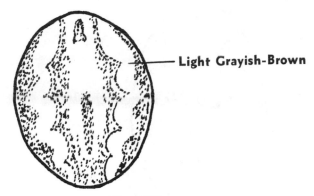

Light Grayish-Brown

**Fig. 152**
**Aranea frondosa.**

sisting of an orb combined with an irregular net; retreat a large silken tent from which a trapline extends to the center of the round web.

Throughout the United States.

*Note:* The following three species of *Araneas* are generally known as the Three House *Araneas* because they are more commonly found about houses, barns, and other outbuildings; however, they also occur on bushes and other plants.

*Aranea sericata. The Gray Cross Spider.* Female from ⅖ to ⅗ inch long; male a little less than ⅓ inch. General color brown tending towards black. This species is the most easily recognized of the three house *Araneas* because it is darker than the other two and because the light lines forming the edges of the folium are broken just in front of the middle of each side, the folium being crossed by a gray patch where the lines are broken and which likely suggested the name of the spider (Fig. 151).

Common about buildings and other wooden structures; rarely found on plants at any distance from a house. Web a complete orb, retreat a dense sheet of silk built across an angle in the building.

Egg sac a large, round, white structure fastened in a sheltered place on the wall of the house and covered with a loose mass of silk threads.

Common in the North but found as far south as Virginia.

*Aranea frondosa. The Foliate Spider.* Female about ⅖ inch long; male slightly smaller. Cephalothorax reddish brown with three longitudinal stripes, one in the middle and one on each side; abdomen light grayish-brown with a darker folium which includes three or more

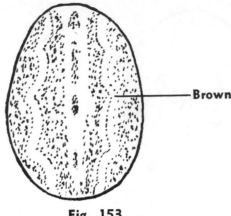

**Fig. 153**
**Aranea ocellata.**

pairs of indistinctly outlined lighter spots (Fig. 152). Name suggested by conspicuous folium.

Found on bushes and herbaceous plants, as well as about houses, where it builds its web with a retreat nearby.

A common species throughout the United States.

*Aranea ocellata.* This spider resembles the foliate spider in appearance though the folium is more dark and uniform in color and less broken by spots and other marks (Fig. 153).

Less common than the other two house araneas and a more northern species.

*Neoscona arabesca.* Female about ⅓ inch long; male about the same. Cephalothorax varies from yellow to orange-yellow to brown with three dark stripes not too well defined; abdomen commonly light yellow with brown markings though sometimes thickly spotted with red, with a row of light spots in the middle, sometimes united into a stripe, and on each side of this a row of dark spots nearly surrounded by lighter color; lower surface of abdomen with a dark center and two or three pairs of yellow spots; sternum bright yellow in the middle; legs with gray or brown rings at the ends of the segments (Fig. 154). Male marked like female.

Lives in tall grass and in bushes; frequently in damp situations as along the shore of a lake or stream. Web a nearly vertical complete orb, six to eighteen inches in diameter; sometimes with a retreat with a trapline leading to the web.

Throughout the United States.

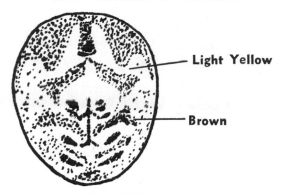

**Fig. 154**
**Neoscona arabesca.**

*Neoscona domiciliorum.* This is a somewhat larger species than *arabesca,* the female measuring from ⅖ to ⅗ inch long, with a triangular-oval abdomen, but similar to *arabesca* in color and markings.

In open woods.

Throughout the United States.

*Neoscona pratensis.* Female from ⅓ to ⅖ inch long; male slightly smaller. Cephalothorax dull yellow or yellowish-brown with a middle and submarginal stripes; abdomen yellowish-brown with a broad middle brown band bordered on each side by a yellow stripe outside of which there is a row of six black spots partly surrounded with yellow; lower surface of abdomen with two curved yellow marks which may be broken into spots; sternum with a yellow stripe in the middle; legs colored like cephalothorax, sometimes a little darker towards the ends of the segments (Fig. 155).

Lives in grass and low bushes where it builds its web.

Found throughout the greater part of the United States.

*Mangora gibberosa.* Female from ⅙ to ¼ inch long; male somewhat smaller. Cephalothorax more or less gibbous or convex posteriorly; posterior median eyes larger than laterals; anterior row recurved; median furrow of thorax deep and usually extending to the cervical groove; tibia of (Fig. 156) third pair of legs with a cluster of long feathery hairs on anterior side. Cephalothorax yellow or light greenish-yellow with a narrow black line in the middle; abdomen gray or light yellow to light greenish-gray with two parallel dark lines on the posterior half and three small black spots in front which may sometimes be absent; legs same color as cephalothorax and armed with black spine-like hairs (Fig. 157).

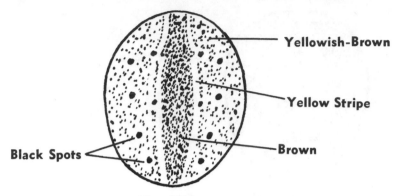

**Fig. 155**
**Neoscona pratensis.**

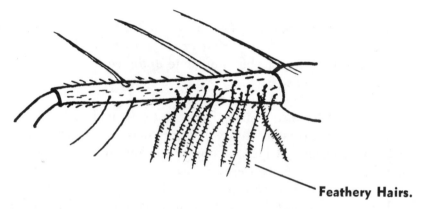

**Fig. 156**
**Tibia of Third Leg of Mangora Showing Cluster of Feathery Hairs.**

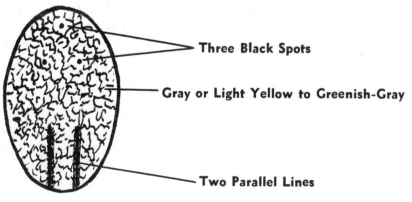

**Fig. 157**
**Mangora gibberosa.**

Lives among grass and bushes in open fields. Web a finely meshed snare, six inches to a foot in diameter, either horizontal or inclined, with sometimes a round opaque screen in the middle that nearly covers the spider.

Throughout the eastern half of the United States west to Nebraska and Oklahoma.

*Mangora placida.* Female ⅙ to ⅕ inch long; male slightly smaller. Structural characteristics as in *gibberosa*. Cephalothorax yellow or brownish-yellow with a brown stripe in the middle and along each side; abdomen white or yellow with a middle brown stripe, narrow in front and wider behind with a row of black spots on the edge of each side and a pair of white spots in the middle; legs same color as cephalothorax though a little darker towards the ends of the segments (Fig. 158).

Lives in grass and bushes in wooded areas. Web a fine meshed snare.

Throughout the eastern half of the United States.

*Mangora maculata.* Female nearly ⅕ inch long; male ⅛. Similar to *gibberosa* but lacks the lines on the cephalothorax and abdomen with several pairs of black spots on the posterior part of the abdomen.

In bushes in wooded areas.

Throughout the eastern half of the United States.

*Larina (Drexelia) directa.* Female ⅖ inch long; male ⅕ inch. Elongated in form, abdomen two or three times as long as wide; abdomen projects over cephalothorax in a blunt point; lateral eyes nearly equal in size and those on each side close together, posterior median eyes near together but the anterior medians widely separated making the median

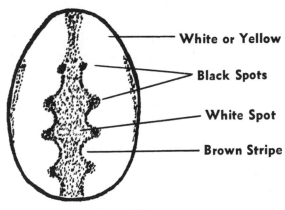

**Fig. 158**
**Mangora placida.**

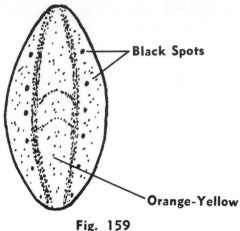

**Fig. 159**
**Larina directa.**

ocular area twice as wide in front as behind. Cephalothorax yellowish with a faint brown median longitudinal line; abdomen orange-yellow and quite variable in markings but usually with six pairs of black spots extending its entire length, the spots sometimes so small as to be hardly visible, at other times so large as to be the distinctive character of the spider; in some individuals the first and third pair of spots are very large, the others very small; sternum yellow; lower surface of

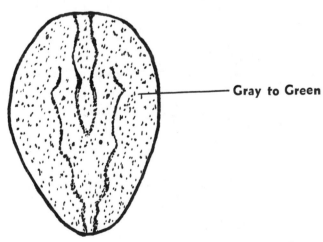

**Fig. 159A**
**Acacesia foliata.**

abdomen with two parallel dark stripes; individuals with spots on abdomen also have legs spotted (Fig. 159).

Lives in grass and herbaceous plants in sunny situations. Web oblique.

A southern species, occurring from North Carolina south to Florida and west to Arizona.

*Acacesia foliata.* Female ¼ inch long; male a little smaller. Median furrow of cephalothorax longitudinal extending forward to the cervical groove; abdomen an elongate rhomboid; second row of eyes strongly recurved; median ocular area not much wider in front than behind, posterior eyes not close together, anterior medians farther from laterals than the laterals are from each other; legs with very few spines. Cephalothorax greenish-gray to brown; abdomen gray to green with black and white lines; legs same color as cephalothorax (Fig. 159A).

In bushes of shaded woods.

New England south to Florida and west to Illinois and Texas.

*Eustala anastera.* Female from ¼ to ⅜ inch long; male somewhat smaller. Abdomen triangular in outline, wide in front bluntly pointed behind; second row of eyes strongly recurved, anterior median eyes farther from the lateral eyes than the laterals are from each other; front legs half longer than the body. Cephalothorax gray, darker at the sides, sometimes with a few black spots; abdomen commonly gray with a tapering scalloped middle stripe and a distinct dark middle spot and two large light spots in the front but this pattern is variable; legs irregularly marked with rings and spots, femora dark toward the end (Fig. 160).

In low trees and among shrubs and bushes, the colors of the spider

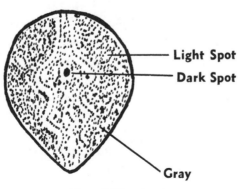

**Fig. 160**
**Eustala anastera.**

being highly protective, resembling the bark of the tree or other plant on which it rests. Web vertical and made in low bushes.

Throughout the United States.


# THE SPINY-BELLIED SPIDERS

*Subfamily Gasteracanthinae*

The spiders of this subfamily are well-named because their abdomens are armed with prominent spines. They have short legs with which they hang in the center of their webs where they look somewhat like wood chips, bits of leaves, and fruits of various plants. In addition to the spines, another striking feature of these spiders is that the spinnerets are elevated on a very conspicuous projection.

*Gasteracantha cancriformis*. Female about ⅓ inch long. The remarkable shape (Fig. 161) and strongly contrasting colors make this spider easy to identify. The ground color is yellow or orange marked with black spots and the abdomen is fringed with six spines.

Lives in shrubs and trees. Web a complete orb, either vertical or inclined, and built between the branches of a tree or shrub.

A southern species found in the Gulf States.

*Micrathena sagitta*. Female about ¼ inch long; male about ⅙ inch. Abdomen arrow-shaped, narrow in front and terminated behind in two large spreading spines with a pair of smaller spines on the front and a spine near the middle of each side (Fig. 162). Cephalothorax light brown or yellowish-brown with white edges; abdomen white or bright yellow spotted with black above and somewhat darker below with black bands and yellow spots; spines black at the points and red at the base; legs same color as cephalothorax.

Found on bushes in open woods. Web a symmetrical inclined orb and often with a short stabilimentum above the hub.

Throughout the eastern half of the United States.

*Micrathena gracilis*. Female somewhat more than ¼ inch long; male somewhat smaller. Abdomen with five pairs of spines, the first near the base, the second nearly midway of its length, and the remaining three pairs at the posterior end. Colors are white, yellow and brown in spots and marks like those of *sagitta* but some individuals are all white and others almost entirely black (Fig. 163). Male with a long slender abdomen without spines.

In wooded areas.

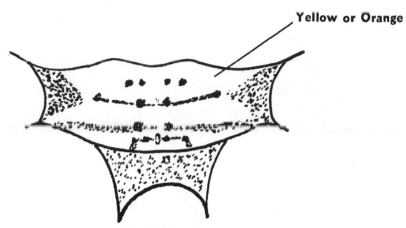

Yellow or Orange

Fig. 161
Gasteracantha cancriformis.

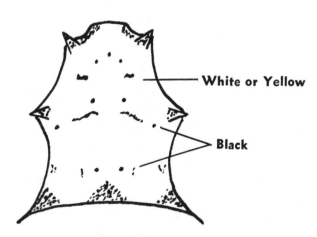

White or Yellow

Black

Fig. 162
Micrathena sagitta.

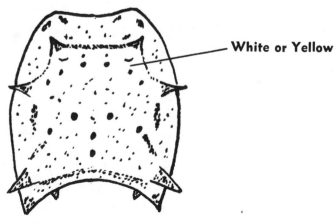

White or Yellow

Fig. 163
Micrathena gracilis.

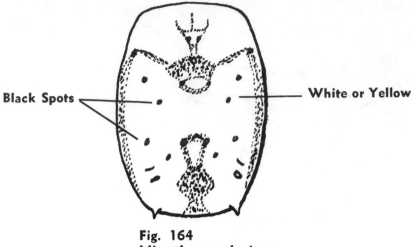

**Black Spots**                    **White or Yellow**

**Fig. 164**
**Micrathena reduviana.**

Common throughout the eastern half of the United States.
*Micrathena reduviana*. Female about ⅙ to ⅕ inch long. Abdomen a
little narrowed in front, truncated behind, with two pairs of comparatively small spines at the posterior end, one below the other.
Cephalothorax brown; abdomen white or yellow with two or three
pairs of black spots along the middle and five or six dark elongated
spots along the sides with the lower surface black mixed with yellow
spots; legs brown (Fig. 164).
  Woods.
  Throughout the Eastern States.


## THE RAY SPIDERS

*Family Theridiosomatidae*

  The ray spiders are small spiders in which the eyes are dissimilar
in color, the tarsi of the fourth pair of legs are furnished with numerous
serrated bristles, and the middle spinnerets are situated between the
hind pair, the four forming a straight transverse line. As these spiders
spin an orb web they are considered by some araneologists to be a
subfamily of the Araneidae but as they have diverged rather sharply
from the more typical orb weavers it appears that they merit a family
of their own.

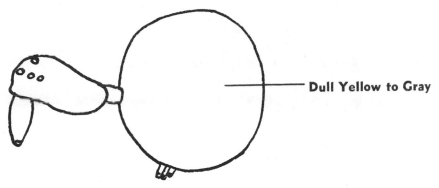

Dull Yellow to Gray

**Fig. 165**
**Theridiosoma radiosa.**
**Side View of Cephalothorax and Abdomen of Female.**

*Theridiosoma radiosa. The Ray Spider.* Female ⅒ inch long; male ⅟₁₂ inch. Cephalothorax heart-shaped, truncate at the base, head much elevated; abdomen rounded, oval, and highly arched. Color varies from a dull yellow to gray with the abdomen marked with silvery spots (Fig. 165).

Prefers damp situations, most commonly found near streams and in moist woodlands. Web often made on the face of a cliff over water. Web differs from usual orb in that the radii, instead of all converging on one center, are united in groups of three or four, each group being connected with the center by a single thread.

Egg sac light brown, pear-shaped, papery and suspended by a thread (Fig. 22).

Maine south to Georgia and west to the Mississippi River.

## THE MIMETIDS

*Family Mimetidae*

The spiders of this family may easily be distinguished from other spiders by the presence on the tibiae and metatarsi of the first two pairs of legs of a series of very long spines regularly spaced and a series of much shorter spines between each two long spines, the short spines being curved and the members of each series being successively longer and longer (Fig. 29).

The mimetids are delicately marked with dark lines and spots, are

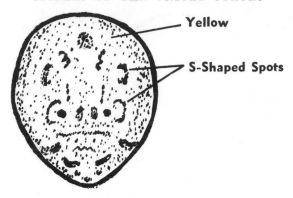

**Fig. 166**
**Mimetus interfector.**

slow-moving, and are found on low plants and bushes as well as under rubbish on the ground. They do not spin a snare but invade the webs of other spiders on which they feed, in fact, from some accounts they appear to eat spiders exclusively and do not prey on insects at all.

*Mimetus interfector.* Female about ¼ inch long; male somewhat smaller. Yellow or pale yellowish in color and variable in markings but typically with a double V-shaped band on the cephalothorax and a series of S-shaped spots on the abdomen with fine transverse lines between them; femora of first two pairs of legs with black spots (Fig. 166).

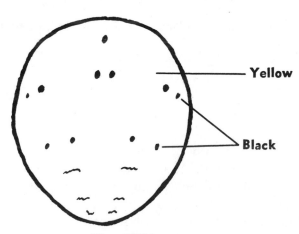

**Fig. 166A**
**Mimetus epeiroides.**

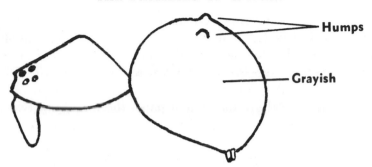

**Fig. 167**
**Ero furcata.**
**Side View of Cephalothorax and Abdomen of Female.**

Egg sac oblong, tapering at both ends, in webs of the spider's victims.

Throughout the eastern half of the United States.

*Mimetus epeiroides.* Female about ¾₁₆ inch long; male slightly less. General color yellow; cephalothorax with four thin black lines extending from the eyes to converge at the dorsal furrow; abdomen with black spots (Fig. 166A).

New England west to Wisconsin.

*Ero furcata.* Female from ⅛ to ⅙ inch long; male slightly smaller. Cephalothorax high in the middle and slopes steeply behind; abdomen with a pair of humps on the highest part. Cephalothorax light yellow, with a broad dark band on each side, and a narrow middle line, crossed by a crescent-shaped mark on the highest part; abdomen grayish with brown spots of various shapes (Fig. 167).

Found in grass and low bushes as well as under stones and leaves on the ground.

Egg sac nearly spherical, pale brown, and enclosed in a loose network of coarse dark reddish threads; suspended by a cord of coarse threads from a support.

Throughout the United States.

## THE CRAB-SPIDERS

*Family Thomisidae*

The members of this family are generally known as crab-spiders because of their superficial resemblance to crabs (Fig. 34). They are short and broad of body, though some of them are long and slender, with legs extended sidewise, crablike, and oddly enough they can walk more readily sidewise and backward than forward. The first and second pairs of legs in the more typical species are much longer and stouter than the third and fourth pairs, the tarsi have two claws, and the eyes are small, dark in color, and arranged in two rows which are almost always recurved.

The Thomisidae do not spin webs but wander about freely on the ground and on plants in search of prey or lie in ambush in a flower where they await the arrival of an unlucky victim, many of them being brightly colored, which aids in their concealment.

The egg sac is lenticular in shape and invariably consists of two equal valves. In most cases after the egg sac is made the female gives up her wandering habits so as to watch it.


## THE MISUMENIDS

*Subfamily Misumeninae*

Most of our crab-spiders belong to this subfamily. They have short, wide bodies and legs that are very unequal in size, the first two pairs being quite long and robust, the last two considerably shorter and weaker. The hairs on the body are filiform or rod-shaped and erect. The misumenids are rather sluggish spiders that have abandoned the wandering habit for a more leisurely sort of life in flower heads and on the ground, where they lie in ambush at which they excel.

*Tamarus angulatus.* Female about ¼ inch long; male slightly smaller. Abdomen rather high, sloping upward toward the posterior end where there is a smaller projection or tubercle; lateral eyes of both rows on tubercles. General color brown mottled with yellow or white, the abdomen crossed by three or four indistinct lines on the posterior half; lower surface of whole body pale without spots except a wide middle band of gray under the abdomen; legs pale (Fig. 168).

Lives on plants, its colors being rather protective.

Throughout the United States.

*Misumena vatia. The Flower Spider.* Female from ⅓ to ½ inch long; male one-fourth to one-third as long as the female. Cephalothorax white to yellow with sides somewhat darker than the middle and the eye region often tinged with red; abdomen usually same color as cephalothorax, without markings as a rule but frequently with a bright

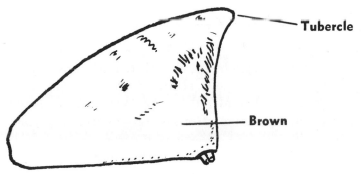

Tubercle

Brown

Fig. 168
Tmarus angulatus.
Side View of Abdomen of Female.

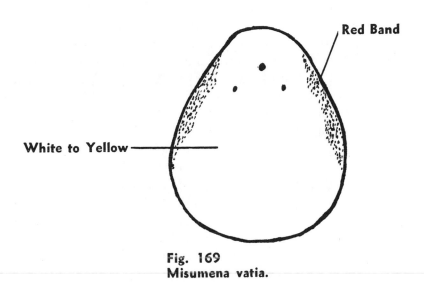

Red Band

White to Yellow

Fig. 169
Misumena vatia.

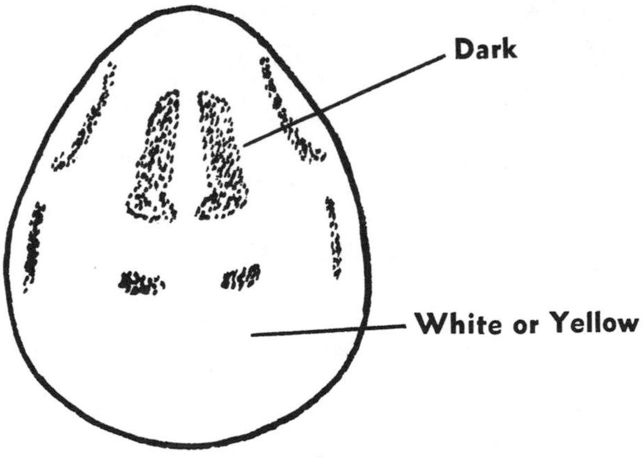

Dark

White or Yellow

Fig. 170
Misumenoides aleatorius.

red band on each side and occasionally with a middle row of spots; legs light colored. Male with cephalothorax dark reddish-brown with a creamy-white spot in the center and abdomen creamy-white with a pair of dorsal and a pair of lateral red bands. This spider is noted for its change of color as it migrates from flowers of differing color (Fig. 169).

Egg sac made upon a leaf, part of the leaf being folded over it and tied with silk as a sort of protective covering.

Throughout the United States.

*Misumenoides aleatorius.* Female about ⅜ inch long; male about ⅛ inch. Cephalothorax relatively flat and a distinct white carina between the eye rows. This species resembles *Misumena vatia* closely and is white or yellow but without the red markings at the sides of the abdomen or between the eyes; abdomen usually without markings except a little gray color in the middle but sometimes with two rows of dark spots. Male with green cephalothorax, yellow abdomen, and first two pairs of legs brown (Fig. 170). Also capable of color change.

Found on flowers.

Throughout the United States.

*Misumenops asperatus.* Female ¼ inch long; male about half as long. Anterior lateral eyes larger than anterior medians. Ground color yellow or white with dull red markings; thorax reddish at the sides; abdomen with a median light red band on the basal half, two bands or rows of spots on the posterior half, and a band on each side; tibiae and tarsi of front legs marked with red rings (Fig. 171). Male like female in color and markings, but the spots are larger and more deeply colored.

Lives in grass and among leaves.

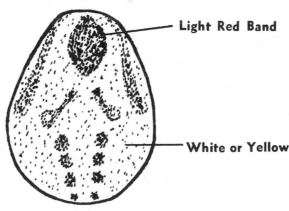

Fig. 171
Misumenops asperatus.

Throughout the United States.

*Oxyptila conspurcata.* Female ⅐ inch long; male slightly smaller. Median ocular area much longer than wide; legs short with few spines, tibiae of first two pairs with two pairs of ventral spines. Cephalothorax reddish-yellow or brown, usually with some silvery-white lines; abdomen irregularly spotted (Fig. 172).

Found under leaves and debris on the ground.

Maine south to Georgia and west to Colorado.

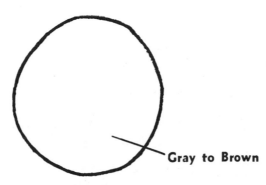

**Fig. 172**
**Oxyptila conspurcata.**

*Coriarachne versicolor.* Female about ¼ inch long; male somewhat smaller. Cephalothorax very flat; anterior row of eyes straight or nearly so with median eyes much smaller than the laterals, posterior row strongly recurved with medians (Fig. 173) smaller than laterals. General color white or yellowish spotted with black and gray, spots varying greatly in different individuals and sometimes so large that the spider is nearly black (Fig. 174).

A common species found on fences, under loose bark, and under stones. The colors of the spider so closely resemble these objects that it is not easily seen.

Throughout the eastern half of the United States.

*Note:* The following species of *Xysticus* are rather crablike in appearance, the abdomen is not much larger than the thorax, and the first and second pairs of legs are a third longer than the third and fourth. The tibia and metatarsi of the anterior legs have generally more than three pairs of spines and the tarsal claws are usually provided with five or six teeth. Median eyes smaller than the laterals; anterior row

**Fig. 173**
**Coriarchne versicolor. Head Showing Arrangement of Eyes.**

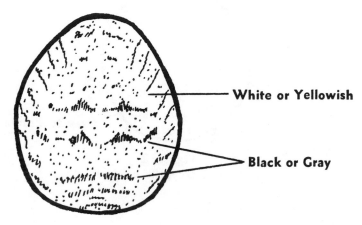

White or Yellowish

Black or Gray

**Fig. 174**
**Coriarchne versicolor.**

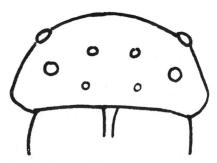

**Fig. 175**
**Xysticus triguttatus.**
**Head Showing Arrangement of Eyes.**

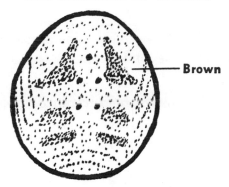

**Brown**

**Fig. 176**
**Xysticus elegans.**

somewhat recurved (Fig. 175). The spiders live under stones, bark, and leaves and some on low plants.

*Xysticus elegans.* Female ⅓ inch long; male ¼ inch. Cephalothorax brownish-yellow with a narrow white marginal line and a light median longitudinal band; abdomen brown with several narrow transverse bands (Fig. 176). Cephalothorax of male reddish-brown, flecked with yellow, and with a broad, light middle band; abdomen brownish-white dotted with brown and with four pairs of brown patches.

Throughout the eastern half of the United States.

*Xysticus gulosus.* Female from ¼ to ⅓ inch long; male ⅕ inch. Grayish-brown in color with indistinct darker markings; entire body cov-

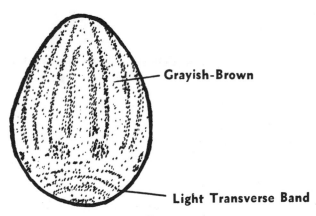

**Grayish-Brown**

**Light Transverse Band**

**Fig. 177**
**Xysticus gulosus.**

ered with fine brown spots; cephalothorax with a light median area and abdomen with light transverse bands on posterior half (Fig. 177).

Usually found under bark and stones which it resembles in color.

Throughout the eastern half of the United States.

*Xysticus nervosus.* Female ¼ to ⅓ inch long; male about ¼ inch. Cephalothorax yellow or brownish-yellow with a broad light band in the middle and a narrow dark line on each margin; abdomen same color, marbled with white and spotted with brown, with three or four pairs of transverse brown bands on posterior half (Fig. 178).

Lives on fences and under bark.

Throughout the East west to the Rockies.

*Xysticus triguttatus.* Female ⅕ inch long; male about ⅙ inch. Cephalothorax brownish-yellow or straw-color with three black spots at the posterior end, which probably suggested its specific name, and indistinct darker bands at the sides; abdomen almost white with a pair of black spots near the base and three or four pairs of more or less broken transverse black stripes on the posterior end. Cephalothorax of male dark brown with a lighter median area and abdomen white with brownish-black markings (Fig. 179).

A very common spider living on grass and low bushes.

Maine south to Georgia and west to the Rockies.

*Xysticus ferox.* Female about ¼ inch long; male about ⅕ inch. Cephalothorax reddish-brown at the sides and yellowish in the middle; abdomen brownish-gray above and white on the sides with several small, black spots on the upper surface in the anterior half and three pairs of black bars on the posterior half; third and fourth pairs of legs with

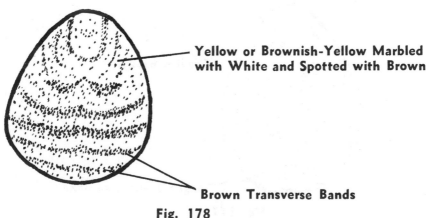

Yellow or Brownish-Yellow Marbled with White and Spotted with Brown

Brown Transverse Bands

Fig. 178
Xysticus nervosus.

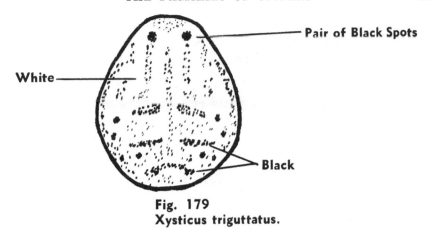

White

Pair of Black Spots

Black

Fig. 179
Xysticus triguttatus.

a distinct dark spot at the ends of femur, patella and tibia (Fig. 180).
Throughout the East.

*Xysticus luctans.* Female from ¼ to ⅓ inch long; male somewhat smaller. Cephalothorax light yellow or reddish-yellow with four narrow brown stripes, one on each side near the margin and the others running back from the lateral eyes, and a brown spot near the hind end and pair of similar spots in the middle; abdomen light gray above with three pairs of black spots, one pair near each end and one in the middle; legs with fine brown spots (Fig. 181).

Throughout the eastern half of the United States.

*Synema bicolor.* Female ⅕ inch long; male somewhat smaller. Median ocular area a little more narrow in front than behind (Fig. 182); tarsal claws of first two pairs of legs (Fig. 183) with more than five or six teeth; tibia of first and second pairs of legs with three pairs of spines. Cephalothorax dark brown to black with a lighter line in the middle and a white line on each side; abdomen light gray with indistinct lighter lines at the sides and small light spots in the middle (Fig. 184).

Found in tall grass and low bushes.

New England to Florida.

*Synema parvula.* Female about ⅛ inch long; male a little less. Structural details as in *bicolor.* Cephalothorax brownish-yellow or yellowish-orange, a little darker at the sides and with a dark brown on the edges over the legs; white rings around the eyes; abdomen white or light yellow with two or three pairs of small brown spots on the anterior half and a wide black or brown band, usually divided by a notch, on the posterior half (Fig. 185).

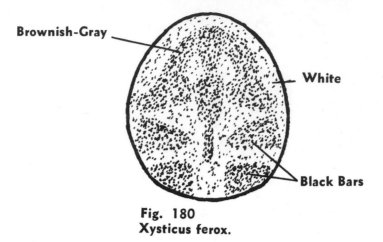

Brownish-Gray

White

Black Bars

Fig. 180
Xysticus ferox.

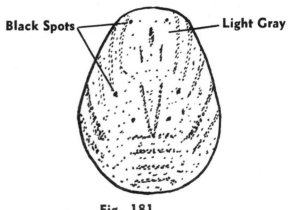

Black Spots

Light Gray

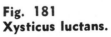

Fig. 181
Xysticus luctans.

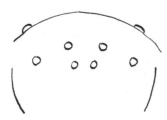

Fig. 182
Synema. Face Showing Arrangement of Eyes.

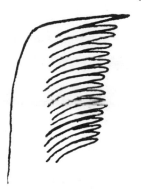

**Fig. 183**
**Tarsal Claws of Synema bicolor.**

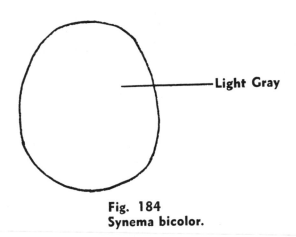

———— Light Gray

**Fig. 184**
**Synema bicolor.**

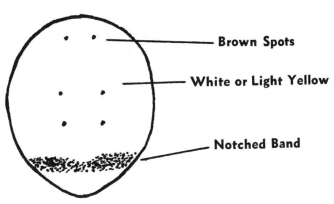

——— Brown Spots

——— White or Light Yellow

——— Notched Band

**Fig. 185**
**Synema parvula.**

Found on flowers, especially the blossoms of the Umbelliferae.

Common in the South Atlantic States but occurring westward to Illinois and California.


## THE PHILODROMIDS

*Subfamily Philodrominae*

The philodromids are active spiders and pursue their prey with

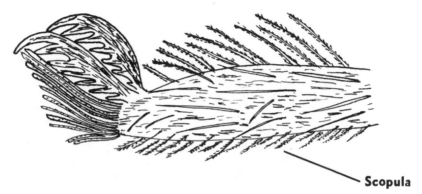

**Fig. 186**
**Tarsus of Philodromus pernix Showing Scopula.**

considerable agility. Most of them live on plants and they are usually colored so that they blend with their surroundings. The tarsi of the first and second pairs of legs are provided with scopulae (Fig. 186) and the third and fourth pairs are as long or nearly as long as the first two.

*Note:* In the following species of *Philodromus* the body is flat and the abdomen is pointed behind. The posterior median eyes are much farther from each other than from the lateral eyes and the posterior eyes are in a slightly recurved line. Quite often the whole body is covered with fine flattened hairs. The egg sac of some species is a glistening white object that readily attracts attention and is invariably made on the branch of a shrub or tree on which the species lives (Fig. 187).

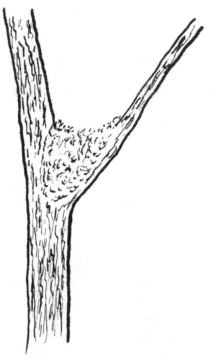

**Fig. 187**
**Egg Sac of Philodromus.**

*Philodromus pernix.* Female about ¼ inch long; male slightly smaller. General color gray, in color the spider resembling an old unpainted building. Cephalothorax darker at the sides with a more or less distinct V-shaped light band on the posterior margin of the head; abdomen with a lanceolate median stripe on the anterior half and a herringbone pattern on the posterior half; legs spotted and darker towards the ends of the segments (Fig. 188). Male colored like the female.

Sometimes found on plants but usually on houses and fences where the spider stands flat against the wall or rail with legs extended sidewise and so closely matching in color the weathered wall or fence that it is not easily detected.

Throughout the United States.

*Philodromus ornatus.* Female about ⅛ inch long; male slightly smaller. Cephalothorax yellowish-white with brown sides; abdomen white with an irregular brown band along each side. Cephalothorax of male orange-brown, darker at the sides; abdomen darker brown and strongly

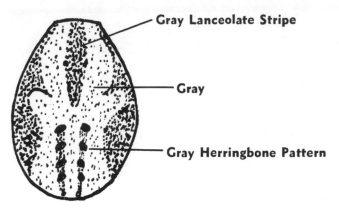

Gray Lanceolate Stripe

Gray

Gray Herringbone Pattern

Fig. 188
Philodromus pernix.

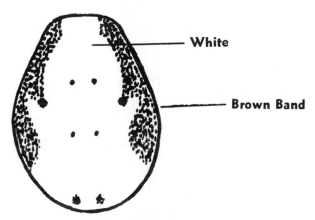

White

Brown Band

Fig. 189
Philodromus ornatus.

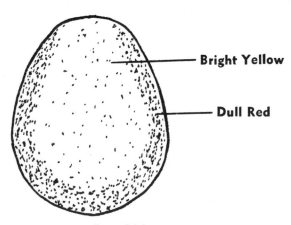

Bright Yellow

Dull Red

Fig. 190
Philodromus rufus.

**Fig. 191**
**Apollaphanes texanus. Cephalothorax.**
**Showing Arrangement of Eyes.**

iridescent with red and green in a bright light; legs orange-brown (Fig. 189).

Throughout the Eastern States.

*Philodromus rufus.* Female about ⅛ inch long; male slightly smaller. Cephalothorax light yellow in the middle, reddish-brown at the sides; abdomen bright yellow in the middle, dull red at the sides; eyes conspicuously ringed in white (Fig. 190).

Found on bushes and trees.

Maine south to Georgia and west to the Rockies.

*Philodromus minutus.* Female ⅛ inch long; male slightly less. Cephalothorax white or yellowish-white, the sides reddish-brown; abdomen a dirty white or yellowish with a median brown stripe on the anterior half and two stripes on the posterior half.

This spider is of more than passing interest because of the curious way it cares for its eggs. It makes an egg sac near the tip of a leaf, then folds the tip with the egg sac back and fastens it to the leaf with many threads of silk, where it remains on guard.

Northeastern States.

*Apollophanes texanus.* Female about ¼ inch long; male slightly smaller. Cephalothorax almost circular; posterior row of eyes strongly recurved, eyes equidistant, anterior laterals equidistant from anterior medians and posterior medians forming with them on each side an equilateral triangle (Fig. 191). Cephalothorax yellowish, slightly mottled with brown on sides; abdomen pale with a brown spear-mark at the base and two more or less connected rows of blackish spots behind.

Southwestern States.

*Ebo latithorax.* Female ⅛ inch long; male slightly smaller. Thorax wider than long; head narrow and rounded in front; posterior row

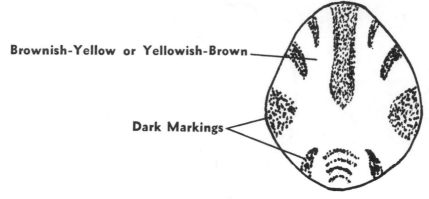

Fig. 192
Ebo latithorax.

of eyes almost straight; second pair of legs more than twice as long as any of the others. Cephalothorax reddish-yellow or yellowish-brown marked with dark brown spots; abdomen brownish-yellow or yellowish-brown flecked with dark on the sides (Fig. 192).

Maine south to Virginia and west to Illinois and Oklahoma.
*Thanatus lycosoides.* Female from ¼ to ⅓ inch long; male a little smaller. Fourth pair of legs longer than first pair; cephalothorax but little if at all longer than wide; anterior lateral eyes closer to anterior medians than to posterior medians. Cephalothorax reddish-yellow with

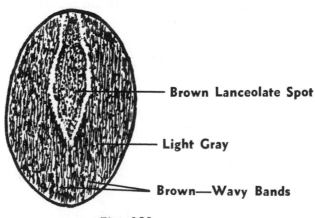

Fig. 193
Thanatus lycosoides.

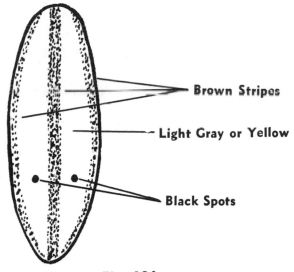

Brown Stripes

Light Gray or Yellow

Black Spots

Fig. 194
Tibellus duttoni.

a central, longitudinal brown band tapering to a point behind and with sides streaked with brown and red; abdomen light above with a slender, brown, lancelike spot in front which reaches beyond the middle and with a wavy band on each side of the posterior part; entire body hairy with longer and darker hairs scattered among the short ones (Fig. 193).

Lives on plants.

Throughout the United States.

*Tibellus duttoni.* Female about ½ inch long; male about ⅓ inch. Body long and slender, cephalothorax much longer than wide, and abdomen very long and nearly cylindrical though somewhat pointed behind; both rows of eyes strongly curved. Light gray or yellow with three longitudinal brown stripes extending the whole length of the cephalothorax and abdomen; on the abdomen one-third of its length from the posterior end is a pair of small round or oval black spots; legs light gray (Fig. 194).

Lives on grass and bushes.

New England south to Florida and west to the Mississippi.

*Tibellus oblongus.* Similar to *duttoni* but not quite as slender with comparatively shorter legs and also found on grass and bushes.

Throughout the United States.

## THE GIANT CRAB-SPIDERS

*Family (Sparassidae) Heteropodidae*

We have within the limits of the United States a small group of essentially tropical or subtropical spiders that resemble the typical small crab spiders in the form of the body and in the manner in which they hold their legs and which because of their large size are generally known as the giant crab-spiders.

*Heteropoda venatoria. The Banana Spider.* Female about an inch long; male slightly smaller. Anterior median eyes smaller than the anterior laterals; clypeus higher than the diameter of an anterior median eye. Cephalothorax yellow to brown with a transverse band of white hairs near the posterior margin; clypeus also with a band of white hairs; abdomen light tan with two or three indistinct longitudinal black lines (Fig. 195).

Found under bark and in similar situations in the open but also in houses, barns and other buildings.

Egg sac a flat, cushion-like affair carried by the female beneath her body.

Florida and the Southwest but often found in bunches of bananas in fruit stores throughout the rest of the country, hence its name of banana spider.

*Olios fasciculatus.* Female an inch or more long; male somewhat smaller. Anterior median eyes as large as or larger than the anterior laterals; clypeus lower than the diameter of an anterior median eye.

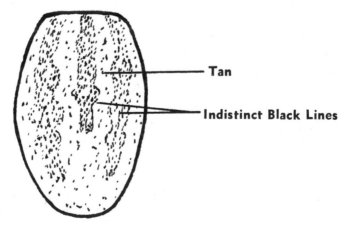

**Fig. 195**
**Heteropoda venatoria.**

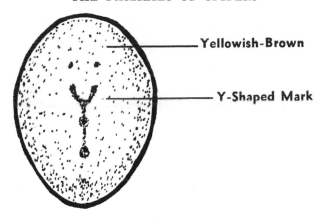

**Fig. 196**
**Olios fasciculatus.**

Cephalothorax reddish-brown or orange; abdomen yellowish-brown with a Y-shaped black mark extending the length of the upper surface, and with several pairs of dark spots on each side of the mark (Fig. 196).

New Mexico, Arizona, Utah, and California.

## THE WANDERING SPIDERS

*Family Ctenidae*

The ctenids wander about in search of prey, many of them over the foliage, others over the ground. Some of them, being covered with dense coats of tawny or brownish hair, resemble the wolf spiders. They are more common in the warmer parts of the United States.

*Ctenus hibernalis.* Female about ½ inch or more long; male somewhat smaller. First row of eyes strongly recurved, eyes in three rows, anterior laterals smaller than anterior medians; two tarsal claws. Tawny with a median longitudinal yellowish band extending over both the cephalothorax and abdomen.

Southern states.

*Anahita punctulata.* Both sexes about ¼ inch long and similar in appearance. Eyes in three rows, anterior medians much smaller than posterior medians. Cephalothorax pale yellowish brown marked with two longitudinal blackish lines and two faint scalloped ones on each

side; abdomen much the same color; legs pale yellowish brown.
     Found in woods and ravines.
     Southern states.


## THE CLUBIONIDS

*Family Clubionidae*

The spiders of this family either live in flat tubular retreats in

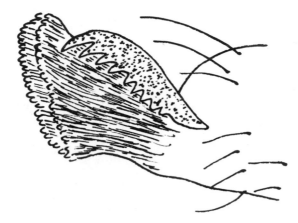

**Fig. 197**
**Tip of Tarsus of Clubiona.**

rolled up leaves or on the ground under stones and rubbish and in
moss. They have eight eyes arranged in two rows, with the anterior
spinnerets close together, and have two tarsal claws. The tarsi are
usually provided with bundles of terminal tenent hairs which, being
dark in color, are quite conspicuous in the light colored species (Fig.
197). There are five subfamilies although the first is regarded as a
distinct family by some araneologists.


## THE ANYPHAENIDS

*Subfamily Anyphaeninae*

The anyphaenids are spiders of average size, generally of pale

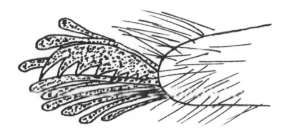

**Fig. 198**
**Tip of Tarsus of Aysha Showing Tufts of Lamelliform Hairs.**

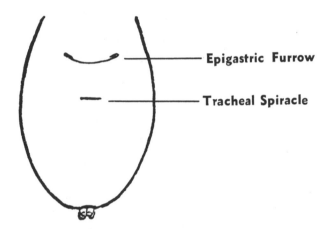

Epigastric Furrow

Tracheal Spiracle

**Fig. 199**
**Lower Surface of Abdomen of Aysha.**

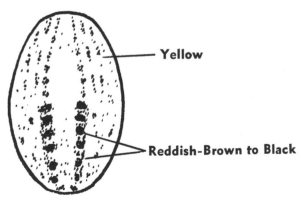

Yellow

Reddish-Brown to Black

**Fig. 200**
**Aysha gracilis.**

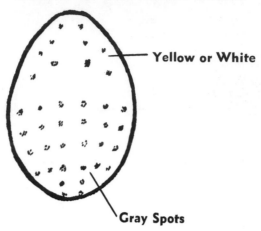

Fig. 201
Anyphaenella saltabunda.

coloration, and differ little from other members of the family in general appearance. They do differ, however, in that the tracheal spiracle is remote from the spinnerets, usually in the middle of the abdomen, and that the claw tufts consist of lamelliform hairs (Fig. 198), these hairs in the other clubionids being broom-shaped.

*Aysha gracilis.* Female ⅓ inch long; male about the same size. Furrow of spiracle much nearer to epigastric furrow than to the spinnerets (Fig. 199); anterior median eyes about equal in size to the lateral eyes; general color yellow, cephalothorax darker than abdomen; cephalo-

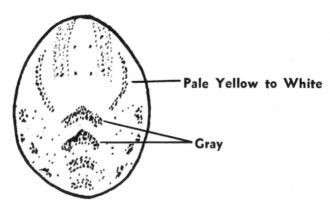

Fig. 202
Anyphaena celer.

thorax with a pair of grayish bands; abdomen with two indistinct rows of reddish-brown to black spots (Fig. 200). Male similar in color.

Lives in silken tubes in rolled leaves of shrubs and herbaceous plants.

Maine south to Florida and west to Nebraska and Oklahoma.

*Anyphaenella saltabunda.* Female ⅛ to ⅕ inch long; male somewhat smaller. Furrow of spiracle about midway between epigastric furrow and spinnerets; anterior median eyes smaller than the laterals; tibia of first pair of legs much longer than carapace, in the female the first pair of legs are twice the length of the body, in the male three times. General color pale yellow or white, the cephalothorax with two broken gray stripes, the abdomen with several rows of gray spots (Fig. 201).

Maine south to Georgia and west to the Mississippi.

*Anyphaena celer.* Female about ⅕ inch long; male slightly smaller. Furrow of spiracle about midway between epigastric furrow and spinnerets; posterior row of eyes lightly procurved, anterior medians smaller than laterals. General color pale yellow to white, the cephalothorax with two broken gray stripes and the abdomen with two longitudinal rows and several transverse rows of gray spots (Fig. 202).

Throughout the East.

## THE CLUBIONIDS

*Subfamily Clubioninae*

In the spiders of this subfamily, the furrow of the spiracle is near the spinnerets, the last segment of the hind spinnerets is conical, and the labium is usually much longer than broad.

*Marcellina piscatoria.* Female about ¼ inch long; male only slightly smaller. Posterior row of eyes procurved, anterior medians much larger than anterior laterals (Fig. 203); cephalothorax yellowish-brown; abdomen brown to gray, sometimes nearly white; legs yellowish-brown.

Spins a silken retreat beneath stones.

New England south to Florida and west to Alabama.

*Note:* The following species of *Clubiona* are of medium or small size, generally white, gray or tawny, with the abdomen unmarked but covered with short hairs that give them a silky reflection. The posterior eyes are equidistant or the median eyes are farther from each other than from the lateral eyes; hind legs longer than the front ones; tibiae

**Fig. 203**
**Marcellina picatoria. Head Showing Arrangement of Eyes.**

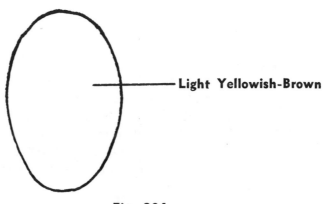

**Fig. 204**
**Clubiona abbotti.**

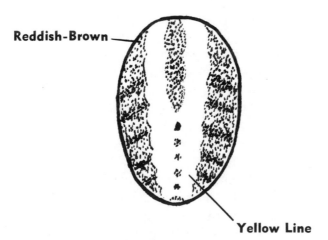

**Fig. 205**
**Clubiona riparia.**

and metatarsi of first two pairs of legs with paired spines; tarsal claws long; and claw tufts conspicuous. The spiders live on plants on which they run rapidly and make silken tubular retreats under bark or in rolled leaves. They winter under bark and stones.

*Clubiona abbottii.* Female from ⅙ to ⅕ inch long; male somewhat smaller. Cephalothorax light yellowish-brown; abdomen same color but lighter (Fig. 204).

One of the most common of the smaller species.

Maine south to Georgia and west to the Rockies.

*Clubiona riparia.* Female ⅓ to ½ inch long; male smaller. This is one of the few *Clubionas* with markings on the abdomen by which it can easily be recognized. Abdomen reddish brown with a central dark stripe broken into spots behind and bordered by pale yellow and with oblique light and dark transverse markings on the sides (Fig. 205).

This spider lives in tall grass and folds a blade to make a three-sided chamber which it lines with silk and which it uses to hide its egg sac.

Maine south to Maryland and west to Illinois.

*Clubiona pallens.* Female about ⅓ inch long; male somewhat smaller. This is another well-marked species which can be distinguished from other *Clubionas* by the markings on the abdomen. Cephalothorax light yellow; abdomen white sometimes with a yellow mark at the basal end and with a middle row of gray spots and a row of larger transverse spots on the sides at the posterior end; legs more deeply colored with

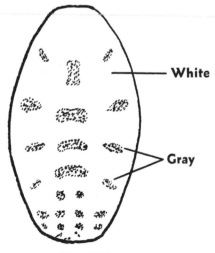

**Fig. 206**
**Clubiona pallens.**

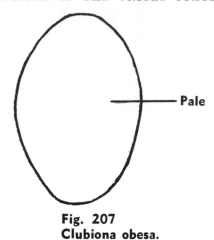

**Fig. 207**
**Clubiona obesa.**

yellow than in other species (Fig. 206).

Usually found under dead leaves, stones, and loose bark.

Maine south to Georgia and west to the Mississippi.

*Clubiona obesa.* Female about ¼ inch long; male about the same or slightly smaller. General color pale without any markings though a median longitudinal stripe may sometimes be faintly indicated on the anterior half (Fig. 207).

New England south to North Carolina and west to Nebraska and Oklahoma.

*Chiracanthium inclusum.* Female about ⅓ inch long; male smaller.

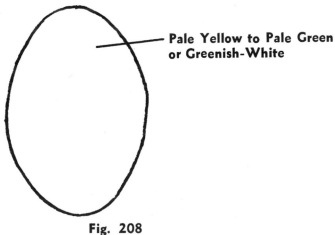

**Fig. 208**
**Chiracanthium inclusum.**

Cephalothorax somewhat convex; posterior median eyes slightly nearer to each other than to the posterior laterals; thoracic groove absent; anterior legs longer than posterior, first two pairs of legs with but few and not paired spines. General color pale yellow to pale green or greenish-white with chelicerae a dark brown (Fig. 208).

A common spider usually found living in a tube of white silk among the leaves of shrubs.

Throughout the United States.

## THE LIOCRANIDS

*Subfamily Liocraninae*

The spiders of this subfamily have the tibiae and metatarsi of the

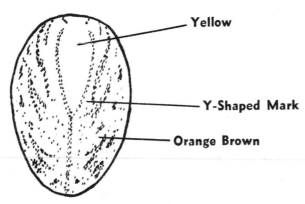

**Fig. 209**
**Zora pumila.**

first two pairs of legs armed with a definite double series of long spines.

*Syspira eclectica.* Female about ½ inch long; male somewhat smaller. Posterior row of eyes recurved, lateral eyes of each side close together, anterior medians much larger in size than anterior laterals. Cephalothorax dusky yellow; abdomen dusky gray; legs yellow with brown rings.

Southwestern states.

*Zora pumila.* Female about ¼ inch long; male somewhat smaller. Posterior row of eyes strongly recurved; tibiae and metatarsi of the first two pairs of legs with many very long spines. General color yellow with orange-brown markings; cephalothorax with two longitudinal bands, each extending backwards from a posterior lateral eye, and a curved band near each edge; abdomen with a Y-shaped mark and two lines of minute dots on the side; legs spotted, the spots being so close together on the patellae and tibiae that these segments appear quite brown (Fig. 209). (This species has been placed in the family *Ctenidae* by some araneologists.)

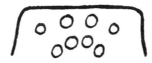

**Fig. 210**
**Agroeca pratensis.**
**Head Showing Arrangement of Eyes.**

Found under stones.
New England south to Alabama.
*Agroeca pratensis.* Female ⅕ to ¼ inch long; male somewhat smaller. Both rows of eyes procurved (Fig. 210), eyes of anterior row close together, those of the second row farther apart; cephalothorax wide behind, low in front, highest near the dorsal groove; abdomen widest across the posterior third; fourth pair of legs longest. Cephalothorax light brownish-yellow with a fine dark line on each side and dusky blotches extending along the radial furrows; abdomen orange-brown with two rows of gray oblique markings; legs light brownish-yellow (Fig. 211). Male similar to female.
Lives among leaves and short grass.
Maine south to Georgia and west to the Rockies.
*Phrurotimpus alarius.* Female about ⅙ inch long; male about ⅛ inch. Anterior row of eyes procurved, eyes large for so small a spider; tarsal claws with small bundles of from six to ten spatulate hairs; tibia and metatarsus of first two pairs of legs with two rows of strong spines on lower side (Fig. 212); legs long and slender. Cephalothorax light yellowish with a narrow black marginal line and two light gray stripes;

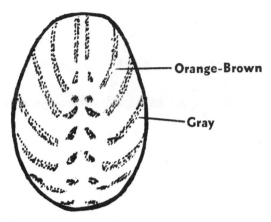

**Fig. 211**
**Agroeca pratensis.**

abdomen gray with several light transverse bands or chevrons which vary greatly in size and shape in different individuals; body usually with iridescent scales; legs pale, except the patella and tibia of first pair which are black or dark gray with the tip of the tibia strongly contrasting white (Fig. 213).

Lives under stones and among moss or short grass in open ground, very active, and can run for a short distance with surprising swiftness.

Egg sac flat, circular in outline, bright red in color and tightly attached to the underside of a stone.

**Fig. 212**
**Phrurotimpus alarius.**
**Front Leg Showing Spines.**

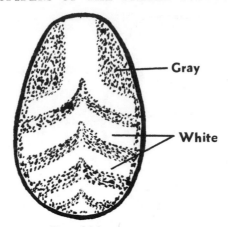

**Fig. 213**
**Phrurotimpus alarius.**

Maine south to Georgia and west to Nebraska and Oklahoma.
*Phrurolithus formica.* Female about ⅙ inch long; male the same length.
Eyes of first row slightly but distinctly narrower than second. Cephalothorax reddish-brown, sometimes with indistinct darker markings, abdomen the same color or black, the upper surface covered with a
shining chitinous plate; legs brown.

Lives under stones or debris and in moss, sometimes in ants' nests.
Throughout the eastern United States.


## THE MICARIIDS

*Subfamily Micariinae*

In the spiders of this subfamily the last segment of the hind spinnerets is very short, often indistinct, and the tarsi of the first pair of
legs are quite long.
*Castianeira cingulata.* Female about ⅓ inch long; male about ¼ inch.
Cephalothorax ovate, rather convex, and with a well-marked thoracic
groove; median eyes farther apart from each other than from the
laterals; tibia of first two pairs of legs with two or three pairs of ventral
spines. Cephalothorax and abdomen dark brown to black, the abdomen
with two white transverse bands; femora of all legs striped with black
(Fig. 214).

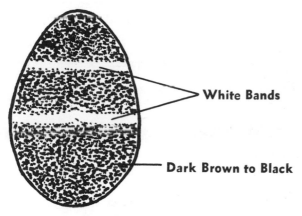

White Bands

Dark Brown to Black

Fig. 214
Castianeira cingulata.

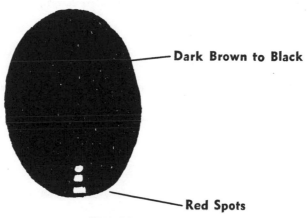

Dark Brown to Black

Red Spots

Fig. 215
Castianeira descripta.

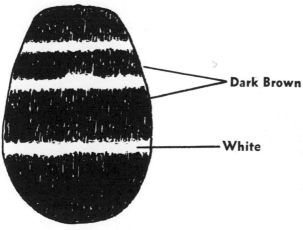

Dark Brown

White

Fig. 216
Castianeira longipalpus.

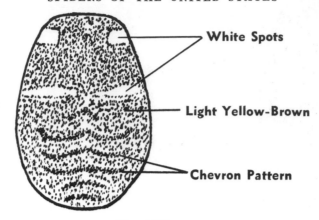

**Fig. 217**
**Micaria aurata.**

Lives on stones and leaves and logs in fields, pastures and wooded areas. Often found associated with ants; indeed, in form and movement resembles the large carpenter ant. Is able to run rapidly when disturbed.

Egg sac a flattened disc, often of an opaline or pearly luster, tough.

Throughout the United States.

*Castianeira descripta.* Female from ⅓ to ⅖ inch long; male nearly ⅓ inch. Structural characters like those of *cingulata*. Cephalothorax and abdomen dark brown to black with or without red markings on

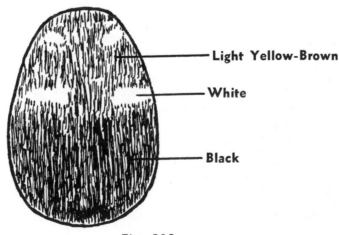

**Fig. 218**
**Micaria longipes.**

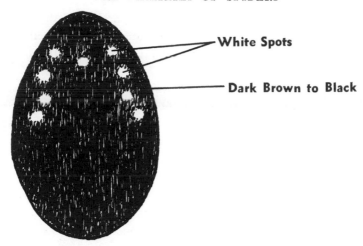

**Fig. 218A**
**Micaria laticeps.**

the abdomen; red markings or spots often restricted to posterior end; femora of legs dark like the cephalothorax but other segments lighter (Fig. 215).

Common under stones in pastures.

Egg sac parchment-like with a metallic luster and attached to stones.

Throughout the United States.

*Castianeira longipalpus.* Female about ⅓ inch long; male about ¼ inch. Structural characters like those of *cingulata.* Cephalothorax light brown; abdomen dark brown with several transverse white stripes, the number varying in different individuals (Fig. 216). More or less resembles *cingulata* but may be distinguished from it by the fact that the legs are banded with black whereas in *cingulata* they are striped with the same color.

Lives under stones and other objects on the ground.

Throughout the East.

*Micaria aurata.* Female about ⅕ to ¼ inch long; male about the same. Thoracic groove absent or faintly indicated and the cephalothorax (usually) and abdomen covered with flattened scales that are iridescent. General color light yellow-brown with gray hairs; abdomen with scales that have red and green metallic reflections, four white spots on the anterior half and a chevron pattern on the posterior half (Fig. 217).

Found in dry and sandy places.

Maine south to Texas but more common in the South.

*Micaria longipes.* This species is similar to *aurata* except that the white spots on the abdomen are thinner and that there is usually no trace of a chevron pattern (Fig. 218).

Throughout the North, west to Nebraska.

*Micaria laticeps.* Female about $\frac{1}{16}$ inch long; male about the same. General color dark brown to black with iridescent scales and spots of white scales (Fig. 218A).

Found under stones in fields and pastures.

New England states.


# THE CORINNIDS

## Subfamily Corinninae

In the spiders of this subfamily the last segment of the hind spinnerets is quite short, the thoracic groove is distinct, and the sternum is margined.

*Trachelas tranquilla.* Female about $\frac{2}{5}$ inch long; male about $\frac{1}{5}$ inch. Cephalothorax almost as wide as long; anterior row of eyes somewhat curved, posterior row much longer and posterior laterals farther from the medians than they are from each other. Cephalothorax dark brown or reddish-brown; abdomen light yellow to light gray with a dark median stripe on basal half and four brown spots on the muscular impressions; legs orange-brown with the first two pairs stouter than the last two (Fig. 219).

Common in dry and warm places, under stones and leaves, at the base of plants and sometimes on fences.

Throughout the United States.


# THE FUNNEL-WEB SPIDERS

## Family Agelenidae

The agelenids or funnel-web spiders spin sheet or platform-like webs which are usually provided with a tubular retreat, in which they stay for the most part except when they emerge and run over the upper surface of the web to seize an insect that has fallen on it. Though more or less sedentary in habits they are rather active and

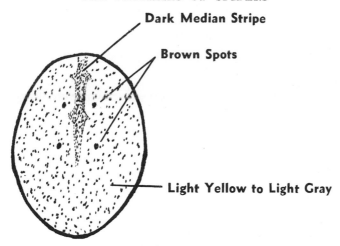

Dark Median Stripe

Brown Spots

Light Yellow to Light Gray

**Fig. 219**
**Trachelas tranquilla.**

good hunters though this activity is more or less contained within the silken field.

The spiders of this family have three claws, usually eight eyes which are typically arranged in two rows, a nearly always oval and convex cephalothorax, and an oval abdomen with spinnerets that are as a rule quite long. The legs are long and thin, especially in the more active species, and the entire body is covered with plumose hairs.

*Cybaeus giganteus.* Female nearly ½ inch long; male about the same. Fore spinnerets contiguous; posterior row of eyes more or less straight. Cephalothorax dark, reddish-brown, shining; abdomen dark grayish-black, with a short basal median light stripe, and covered with short black hairs.

Eastern states.

*Cybaeus reticulatus.* Female about ½ inch long; male slightly smaller. Spinnerets and eyes as in *giganteus.* Cephalothorax orange-brown with dusky markings; abdomen yellow with black chevrons; legs brown with black rings (Fig. 220).

Found under stones and debris on the ground in wooded areas. Web less funnel-like than other agelenids and spider less active than other species.

Pacific coast states.

*Agelena (Agelenopsis) naevia.** The Common Grass Spider.* Female

* A grayer species, *Agelena pennsylvanica,* is common in open woods and around buildings.

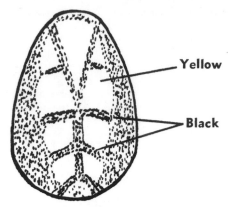

**Fig. 220**
**Cybaeus reticulatus.**

**Fig. 221**
**Agelena naevia.**
**Head Showing Arrangement of Eyes.**

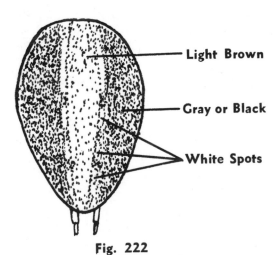

**Fig. 222**
**Agelena naevia.**

from ¾ inch to an inch long; male only slightly smaller. Hind spinnerets long, distal segment about twice as long as the basal; both rows of eyes strongly procurved so that the posterior lateral and anterior median eyes form a nearly straight line (Fig. 221); cephalothorax narrowed in front; legs large and long, the fourth pair almost twice as long as the body. Cephalothorax yellowish to brown with a pair of dark longitudinal bands extending back from the lateral eyes and a black line the edge of each side; abdomen gray or black at the sides and lighter brown in the middle with two rows of white or

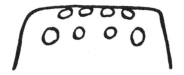

**Fig. 223**
**Calymmaria cavicola.**
**Head Showing Arrangement of Eyes.**

light-colored spots; legs with dark rings at the ends of the segments and lighter rings in the middle of femur and tibia (Fig. 222).

Found usually in open fields. Web flat and shaped according to the surrounding objects to which it is fastened with a tube at one side and often up to three feet in width; built near the surface of the ground in a grassy place, with an irregular open net-work of threads above the sheet that is supported by the stalks of grass that extend above it.

Egg sac disc-like and placed in a secluded situation, often found beneath loose bark on trees and stumps, and closely attached to the supporting object; silk of sac often covered with bits of rotten wood or other debris (Fig. 26).

Maine south to Florida and west to Kansas and Texas.

*Calymmaria cavicola.* Female about ¼ inch long; male about the same size. Anterior row of eyes slightly (Fig. 223) procurved, posterior row slightly recurved, posterior medians smaller than posterior laterals; femora of legs longer than carapace. Cephalothorax yellowish-orange with faint markings; abdomen yellow with indistinct gray chevrons on posterior half; legs yellowish-orange with dark rings (Fig. 224).

Found in dark places in wooded areas; also in caves.

Tennessee, Indiana, Alabama, and Florida.

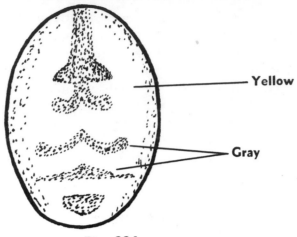

**Fig. 224**
**Calymmaria cavicola.**

*Tegenaria derhami.* Female ⅖ inch long; male slightly smaller. Anterior row of eyes slightly procurved with (Fig. 225) the eyes equal in size or the medians smaller than the laterals, posterior row slightly procurved with the medians only slightly smaller than the laterals; first and fourth pairs of legs nearly twice the length of the body; tibia with two small teeth. Cephalothorax pale or light yellowish-brown with two gray longitudinal stripes; abdomen pale with many irregular gray spots, some more or less connected forming a median band, and others along each side; legs with faint gray rings at the ends of each segment (Fig. 226).

Found under stones and in rock crevices but more commonly in barns, cellars and dark corners of rooms. Web not as flat or as large as that of *Agelenopsis naevia* but with a similar tube. It is often spread under beams and floors, fastened by threads at the sides and edges, and as it gathers dust and other debris hangs down by its own weight and becomes torn and tangled.

**Fig. 225**
**Tegenaria derhami.**
**Head Showing Arrangement of Eyes.**

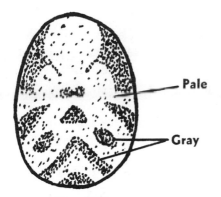

**Fig. 226**
**Tegenaria derhami.**

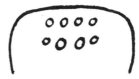

**Fig. 227**
**Coras medicinalis.**
**Head Showing Arrangement of Eyes.**

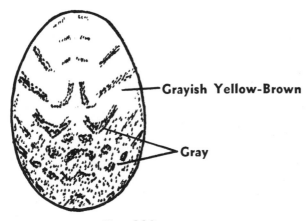

**Fig. 228**
**Coras medicinalis.**

Throughout the United States.

*Coras medicinalis.* Female about ½ inch long; male the same size. Posterior median eyes much larger than anterior (Fig. 227) laterals; head large and wide; abdomen large and oval, widest across the posterior half; upper pair of spinnerets longest. Cephalothorax yellowish-brown, darkest in front with grayish bands; abdomen marked with a series of gray spots of irregular shape, smallest toward the front and larger and darker toward the end; legs faintly ringed with gray (Fig. 228).

Found in hollow trees, under loose bark, in crevices among rocks. Web usually curved in various shapes according to the place where it is built; once thought to be narcotic and used in the treatment of fevers.

Throughout the United States.

*Wadotes calcaratus.* Female nearly ½ inch long; male somewhat smaller. Anterior median eyes much smaller than the laterals; lower margin of chelicera with two teeth. Cephalothorax yellowish-brown; abdomen grayish with a median light stripe in front and a double row of pale markings behind; legs yellowish-brown.

Lives under stones and loose bark.

Maine south to Georgia and west to the Rockies.

*Cicurina robusta.* Female from ⅕ to ¼ inch long; male slightly smaller. Anterior median eyes separate the lateral eyes by a distance exceeding the diameter of these eyes; height of clypeus about equal to the diameter of an anterior lateral eye. Cephalothorax brown or yellowish-brown; abdomen light gray with darker markings; legs same color as cephalothorax (Fig. 229).

Found under stones and leaves in woods. Web a delicate horizontal structure.

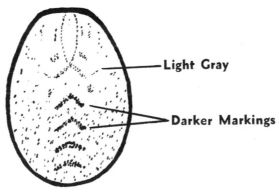

Light Gray

Darker Markings

Fig. 229
Cicurina robusta.

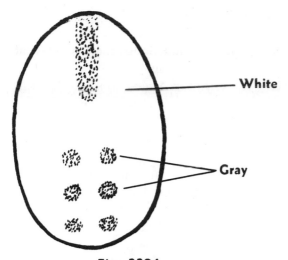

White

Gray

**Fig. 229A
Cicurina brevis.**

**Fig. 230
Cryphoeca montana.
Face Showing Arrangement of Eyes.**

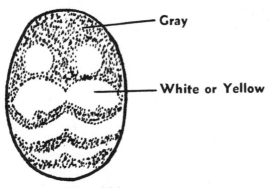

Gray

White or Yellow

**Fig. 231
Cryphoeca montana.**

Widely distributed throughout the United States, especially abundant in the North.

*Cicurina brevis.* Female from ¹⁄₁₆ to ³⁄₁₆ inch long; male somewhat smaller. Cephalothorax yellowish-orange; abdomen white, sometimes with a pattern of gray markings consisting of a median stripe in front and several pairs of spots behind; legs yellowish-orange (Fig. 229A).

Found under stones and dead leaves.

New England south to North Carolina and west to the Mississippi.

*Cryphoeca montana.* Female about ⅙ inch long; male ⅛ inch. Anterior median eyes much smaller than (Fig. 230) the anterior laterals; height of clypeus less than the diameter of an anterior lateral eye. Cephalothorax yellow with a dark marginal stripe and broken radiating dark marks; abdomen gray and yellow marked with a series of chevrons; legs yellow (Fig. 231).

Lives under stones, leaves, and debris on the ground in wooded areas.

New England west to the Mississippi.

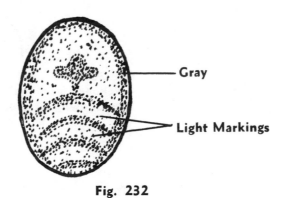

**Fig. 232**
**Hahnia cinera.**

## THE HAHNIIDS

*Family Hahniidae*

The spiders of this family may be recognized by the arrangement of the six spinnerets which are in a more or less single transverse row. They are small in size and spin a delicate sheet web without a retreat near the ground, under stones and leaves and in short thin grass and

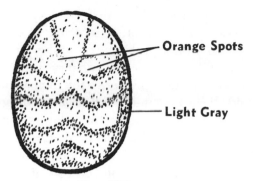

Orange Spots

Light Gray

**Fig. 233**
**Neoantista agilis.**

moss. The web is so delicate that it is not easily seen except when covered with dew when it becomes more visible.

*Hahnia cinera.* Female about $\frac{1}{12}$ inch long; male only slightly smaller. Anterior median eyes smaller than anterior laterals; tracheal spiracle twice as far from the epigastric furrow as from the base of the median spinnerets. Cephalothorax brownish with dark radiating markings; abdomen with a double row of oblique light markings on a gray ground (Fig. 232).

Maine south to North Carolina and west to Utah and Oklahoma.

*Neoantistea agilis.* Female about $\frac{1}{8}$ inch long; male only slightly smaller. Anterior median eyes larger than anterior laterals; tracheal spiracle twice as far from the base of median spinnerets as from the epigastric furrow; carapace nearly as broad as long. Cephalothorax bright orange-brown or reddish; abdomen light gray with many irregular pale spots and a pair of orange-colored spots in the middle; legs yellowish, ringed with gray (Fig. 233).

Maine south to Florida and west to New Mexico.


## THE NURSERY-WEB WEAVERS

*Family Pisauridae*

The pisaurids are wandering spiders which stalk their prey and resemble the wolf spiders closely in appearance though they differ from them in certain habits. Many of them live in moist areas, along the edges of streams and lakes, and some of them are wonderfully adapted to live near or on the water surface, even entering the water to feed on fish; hence they are often referred to as "water spiders" though a better name would probably be "fisher spiders." However, they are more generally known as the "nursery-web weavers" because of the webs the females make as nurseries for their young.

Few of our spiders show as much maternal devotion to their young as do the female pisaurids. From the time the egg sac is made until the eggs are ready to hatch, the female carries it about with her wherever she goes, supported beneath her body. The egg sac is usually so large that the female has to run on the tips of her tarsi to hold it clear of the ground. Just before the spiderlings are ready to emerge from the egg sac or just after they have begun to do so, the female fastens it among the leaves at the top of a herbaceous plant or at the end of a branch of a shrub and then builds a nursery about by tying the leaves together with a network of threads. Here the mother remains on guard, protecting the spiderlings until they have molted and wandered away, perhaps for a week or more.

*Pelopatis undulata.* Female ½ to ¾ inch long; male smaller. Anterior row of eyes so strongly procurved and posterior row so strongly recurved that the eyes appear to be in four rows of two each; median ocular quadrangle (anterior and posterior medians) about as long as broad; cephalothorax much longer than wide; abdomen long and slender; legs very long; tibia of first two pairs of legs with five pairs of ventral spines, metatarsi with four pairs. Cephalothorax dull yellow

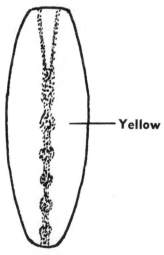

Fig. 234
Pelopatis undulata.

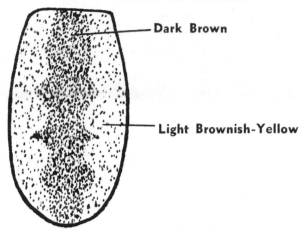

Dark Brown

Light Brownish-Yellow

**Fig. 235**
**Pisaurina mira.**

with a longitudinal thin black line; abdomen yellowish with a dusky longitudinal line that is a continuation of the one on the cephalothorax and which narrows behind with edges gently scalloped; legs light yellowish-brown (Fig. 234).

A southern species occurring from South Carolina south to Florida and west to Texas.

*Pisaurina mira.* Female about ½ inch long; male slightly smaller. Anterior row of four eyes; median ocular area little longer than wide; height of clypeus less than the length of the median ocular area. Extremely variable in color but typically the body is light brownish-yellow with a darker brown broad median band in the middle of both cephalothorax and abdomen the edges being straight on the cephalothorax, undulating on the abdomen (Fig. 235).

Lives in tall grass and bushes.

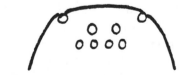

**Fig. 236**
**Dolomedes tenebrosus.**
**Head Showing Arrangement of Eyes.**

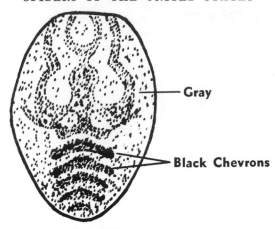

**Fig. 237**
**Dolomedes tenebrosus.**

A common species throughout the eastern half of the United States.

*Note:* In the following species of *Dolomedes* there are four eyes in the anterior row and the median ocular area is as wide as or wider than long (Fig. 236). The Dolomedes quite often attract attention because of their large size and though they are most commonly seen near water or in marshy places they may also be observed in cellars and other dark and dry places.

*Dolomedes tenebrosus. The Dark Dolomedes.* Female about ⅞ inch long; male about half the size. Colors light brown, gray, and black; thorax dark in the middle with light bands on each side that extend around under the eyes and meet in front; abdomen with several black chevrons on the posterior half (Fig. 237); legs indistinctly marked with light and dark rings.

Often found in wooded areas some distance from water.

Throughout the eastern half of the United States.

*Dolomedes scriptus. The Northern Dolomedes.* Female a little smaller than *tenebrosus;* male smaller than female. Cephalothorax brown with a narrow median light line; abdomen with four transverse W-shaped yellow bands; sternum blackish with a yellow median band (Fig. 238).

Maine south to Florida and west to Arizona.

*Dolomedes sexpunctatus. The Six-dotted Dolomedes.* Female from ⅗ to ⅘ inch long; male considerably smaller. Dark greenish-gray or greenish-brown with a white band on each side extending the entire length of the body, two rows of white spots on the upper surface of

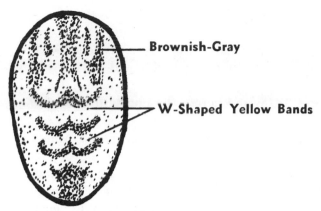

Brownish-Gray

W-Shaped Yellow Bands

Fig. 238
Dolomedes scriptus.

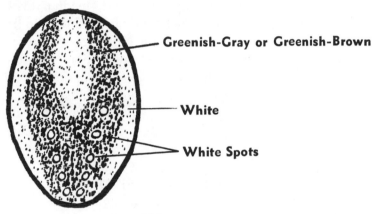

Greenish-Gray or Greenish-Brown

White

White Spots

Fig. 239
Dolomedes sexpunctatus.

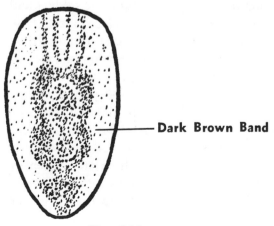

Dark Brown Band

Fig. 240
Timus peregrinus.

the abdomen, and six dark spots on the sternum, whence the name of the spider (Fig. 239).

Common in marshy places and along the edges of ponds where it may be seen running over floating vegetation and diving when frightened.

New England south to Texas and across the northern part of the country to the Pacific Northwest.

*Dolomedes albineus. The Whitish Dolomedes.* This is an ash-gray Southern species that rests with its legs outspread and head downwards on the trunks of cypress and tupelo in the swamplands and is quite motionless until disturbed when it disappears from sight around the trunk of the tree or into the water to skate away or hide beneath the surface.

*Tinus peregrinus.* Female nearly an inch long; male about half the size. First row of eyes lightly procurved, median eyes larger than laterals, median ocular area much wider behind than in front. Cephalothorax light brown to yellow with a broad gray median longitudinal band and dusky stripes along the margin; abdomen with a dark brown middle band margined by narrow light lines; legs reddish-brown; Sternum yellow with three pairs of light gray spots (Fig. 240).

Found in the Southwest, from Arkansas and Texas west to California.


## THE WOLF SPIDERS

*Family Lycosidae*

The wolf spiders, as their name suggests, are hunting spiders that chase their prey. They are among the most common of our spiders and may be seen running through the grass or lurking under stones. Quite adaptable, they occupy almost every variety of terrestrial habitat; some are found near water, others prefer open shifting sands into which they dig tunnels, and still others live among the grass roots.

Their colors are black and white or the color of the ground, stones, and leaves, and in some species the markings are more distinct on the lower surface than on the upper. The legs are fairly long, with the fourth pair the longest, and the first and second pairs are more densely covered with fine hairs and have shorter spines, which are less easily seen, than the third and fourth. The feet have three claws, the under one small and covered by the surrounding hairs. The eyes are in three rows; the first row consists of four small eyes and the two posterior rows each of two large eyes (Fig. 6).

The egg sac, which varies in shape, being spherical in some species, flattened in others, consists of two valves and is carried about by the female attached to the spinnerets by a bundle of threads (Fig. 240A). After hatching the young move to the body of the mother and are carried about by her for some time. A few species spin webs.

*Sosippus floridanus.* Female ⅗ inch long; male only slightly smaller.

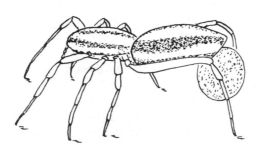

**Fig. 240A**
**Wolf Spider with Egg Sac.**

Anterior row of eyes strongly procurved, laterals being as large as or larger than the medians and set on tubercles, and longer than the second row; tarsi and metatarsi of anterior legs densely scopulate; posterior spinnerets longer than anterior with last segment about as long as the basal. Cephalothorax deep reddish-brown or reddish-black with a median stripe of white or yellow hairs and a wider marginal white band; abdomen brown or blackish with a gray pubescence on each side and with alternating gray and black transverse lines; legs brown with rings of black and white hairs (Fig. 241).

A sedentary spider spinning a large permanent funnel-web on which it runs like the grass spider, *Agelenopsis.*

Common in Florida.

*Note:* The following species of *Lycosa* are among the larger and more familiar members of the family. They may frequently be seen running over the ground in pastures or hiding under stones and debris in fields or along the edges of woods. While some are wanderers, others build retreats which may be merely a shallow excavation under a log or stone, lined with silk and surrounded by a wall of earth or of sticks

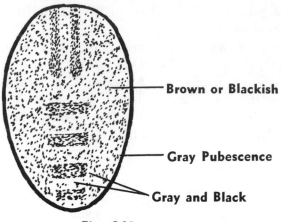

**Brown or Blackish**

**Gray Pubescence**

**Gray and Black**

**Fig. 241**
**Sosippus floridanus.**

and stones, or a vertical tube in the ground, which may be a foot or more in depth and often lined with a thin film of silk. The egg sac is spherical, usually white (sometimes green) at first but turning brown or gray with age or as it is carried about by the female.

*Lycosa helluo.* Female about ¾ inch long; male about ½ inch. General color dull yellow or greenish-brown; cephalothorax with a narrow yellow stripe in the middle and one on each side; abdomen with a longitudinal lanceolate stripe which is wider in the middle and pointed at each end on the anterior half and with a series of indistinct chevrons on the posterior half (Fig. 242).

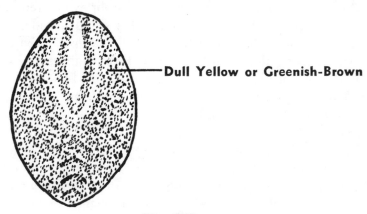

**Dull Yellow or Greenish-Brown**

**Fig. 242**
**Lycosa helluo.**

Lives under stones or other objects on the ground in a shallow nest, lined with silk, usually in the woods. Sometimes the nest is surrounded with a low wall of earth or of sticks and leaves.

One of the most common of the lycosids throughout the East and as far west as Texas and Utah.

*Lycosa riparia.* Cephalothorax brown with a narrow grayish-yellow median band; abdomen grayish-brown with scattered minute spots of black pubescence and an indistinct lanceolate stripe on the anterior half and with several black chevrons on the posterior half.

Usually found on or near water.

A southern species, occurring from the District of Columbia south and westward to Kansas and Texas.

*Lycosa aspersa. The Tiger Wolf.* Cephalothorax dark reddish-brown, blackish about the eyes, with a more or less distinct narrow median stripe and a lighter uneven edged band on each side; abdomen dark with a forked black mark on the anterior half followed by a series of chevrons.

In open woodlands where it digs a tunnel six or seven inches deep in the ground with a parapet of moss and debris and a canopy with an opening on one side and on which are placed bits of soil, moss, and leaves so that the entire nest is well concealed and blends with its surroundings.

New England south to the Gulf of Mexico and west to Kansas.

*Lycosa carolinensis.* Female nearly one and one-half inches long; male about four-fifths. Cephalothorax clothed with brown and gray hairs like the fur of a mouse (lighter in males) and usually without distinct markings; abdomen light brown covered above with long brown to grayish-brown pubescence with a forked median stripe on the anterior half followed by several chevrons and often a series of light dots along each side.

Commonly found in open country often on dry hillsides where the female digs a burrow six or seven inches deep, upper part always inclined and the deeper part sometimes quite tortuous, often with a turret around the entrance. The spider, however, is often found running about on the ground or lurking under stones.

The largest of our wolf spiders and found throughout the greater part of the United States.

*Lycosa avida.* Female ⅖ to ½ inch long; male somewhat smaller. General color from light gray to almost black; cephalothorax with a reddish-yellow or reddish-brown median band which becomes reduced to a narrow stripe between the eyes and a light band on each lateral

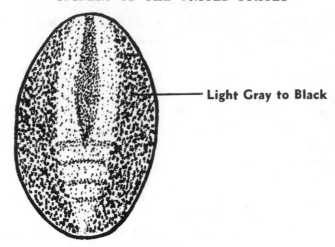

Fig. 243
Lycosa avida.

margin; abdomen with a longitudinal pale band which tapers to a
point at the spinnerets and which encloses a distinct lanceolate mark
sometimes followed by several dark transverse lines; lower surface of
abdomen usually with two black stripes that make a U-shaped figure
(Fig. 243).

A common spider in pastures where it may be seen running in
the grass or hiding under stones.

Throughout the United States.

*Lycosa rabida.* Female ⅘ of an inch long; male ½ inch. Cephalothorax
dark gray with three light longitudinal stripes and a narrow light line
along each margin; abdomen with a broad dark median band notched
on each side and enclosing several pairs of light spots; legs yellowish-
gray, though in the male the first pair of legs are dark brown or black
(Fig. 244).

Maine south to Florida and west to Nebraska and Oklahoma.

*Lycosa punctulata.* Female ⅗ or more of an inch long; male about the
same or perhaps only slightly smaller. Cephalothorax light brown or
yellow with two brownish to black longitudinal stripes which run forward over the eyes, a very narrow marginal line on each side and a
wider submarginal blackish line; abdomen with a brownish to black
longitudinal median band and spots and streaks of brown and grayish-
brown along the sides (Fig. 245).

Throughout the eastern half of the United States west to the
Rockies.

*Lycosa frondicola.* Female about ½ inch long; male ⅗ inch. Cephalo-

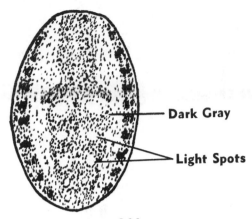

**Fig. 244**
**Lycosa rabida.**

thorax dark brown with a median light band, widest just behind the eyes; abdomen brown or grayish-brown with an indistinct lanceolate stripe and indistinct chevrons on the posterior half (Fig. 246).

Found most often along the edges of woods among the fallen leaves.

Maine south to North Carolina and west to the Rockies.

*Lycosa pratensis.* Female about ½ inch long; male slightly smaller. General color yellowish-brown; cephalothorax with a median light band with two brown spots in the middle; abdomen with a lanceolate stripe followed by four or five chevrons; legs darker toward the ends,

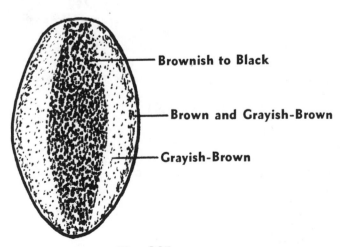

**Fig. 245**
**Lycosa punctulata.**

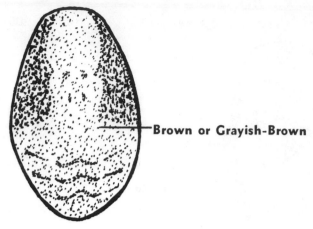

Brown or Grayish-Brown

Fig. 246
Lycosa frondicola.

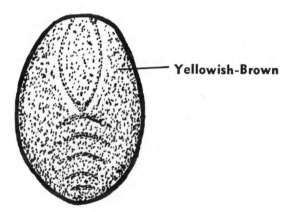

Yellowish-Brown

Fig. 247
Lycosa pratensis.

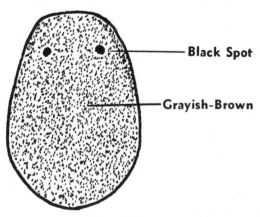

Black Spot

Grayish-Brown

Fig. 248
Lycosa gulosa.

femora with two broken dark bands and patella and tibia of third and fourth pairs with faint dark rings (Fig. 247).

This is not a particularly active spider and is commonly found under stones.

A common species in the Northeast.

*Lycosa gulosa.* Female about ½ inch long; male slightly smaller. Cephalothorax light gray in the middle, dark brown at the sides; abdomen grayish-brown with a darker lanceolate stripe on the anterior half which, however, may be wanting, and with sides darkest toward the front end where there are two black spots; legs gray with two or three indistinct rings on each segment (Fig. 248).

Common in the woods among dead leaves where its brown and gray colors blend with that of the leaves.

Maine south to Georgia and west to the Rockies.

*Geolycosa pikei.* Female about ¾ inch long; male somewhat smaller. Cephalothorax very high in front and usually slopes unbroken to the posterior; dorsal spines absent on the tibia of the fourth pair of legs in the female. Cephalothorax dark reddish-brown to blackish with a light median band; abdomen gray or grayish-brown with a dark brown median band with a series of indentations along each side; first two pairs of legs thicker than the others and more densely covered with hairs (Fig. 249).

This spider digs a burrow, often from ten to twelve inches deep, in a sandy situation, the sand being held in place by silk. Sometimes a turret of bits of stick and straw is built around the entrance but more

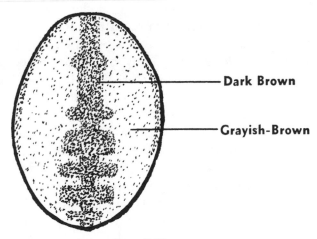

**Fig. 249**
**Geolycosa pikei.**

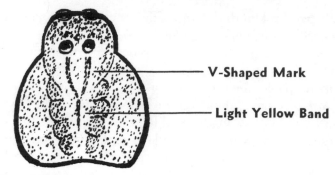

**Fig. 249A**
**Cephalothorax of Pirata Showing Characteristic Pattern.**

often the entrance is left clear and not concealed in any way. The female rarely leaves the burrow, remaining for the most part near the mouth of the opening to await its prey, but is very sensitive to the slightest vibrations of the ground and disappears beneath at the slightest sign of danger. To see the spider it is necessary to remain quiet near the burrow for several minutes or until it returns to the surface.

Eastern and Middle States south to Georgia.

*Tarentula pictilis.* Female about ½ inch long; male about ⅖ inch. First row of eyes shorter than the second; two dorsal spines on tibia of fourth pair of legs about equally stout. Cephalothorax chocolate-brown with a middle grayish band; abdomen dark brown with a black spot on each side at the base, a light spot between each black spot and the middle line, and a series of chevrons on the posterior half.

Found among moss and low shrubs, on mountains.

Northeastern United States.

*Note:* The species of *Pirata* can usually be distinguished from other members of the family by the characteristic pattern on the cephalothorax (Fig. 249A). This consists of a pale or light yellow band extending from the eye region back to the posterior edge and enclosing a dark V-shaped mark. On either side of this median light area the cephalothorax is dark brown, gray, or black to a submarginal light stripe and sometimes a marginal line of white hair. The abdomen may have a lanceolate stripe on the anterior half or it may be wanting but there are usually paired white or yellow spots on the posterior half and sometimes several chevrons near the caudal end. The anterior eyes are in a straight or slightly procurved line and the anterior tibiae are armed with two or three pairs of spines. The Piratas are small or medium-

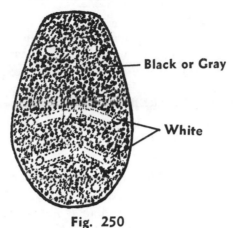

Fig. 250
Pirata minutus.

sized spiders that live in damp fields and in the vicinity of water as along the margins of ponds and streams. The egg sac is white and spherical.

*Pirata minutus.* Female slightly more than ⅛ inch long; male about ⅛ inch or less. Cephalothorax dark brown with a forked reddish-yellow median band and a thin marginal line of white hair; abdomen black or gray with or without a narrow lanceolate stripe with several paired spots of white hair some of which appear to be joined by light transverse lines (Fig. 250).

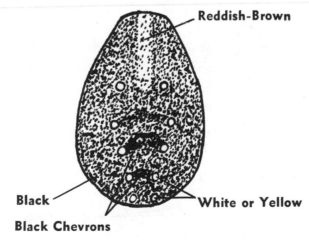

Fig. 251
Pirata montanus.

New England west to Illinois.

*Pirata montanus.* Female slightly more than ⅛ inch long; male about the same. Cephalothorax deep brown or blackish with a forked yellow median stripe and a marginal line of white hair on each side; abdomen black with a reddish-brown median lanceolate stripe on the anterior half, several black chevrons on the posterior half, and with a spot of white or light yellow hair at the lateral ends of each chevron (Fig. 251).

New England west to Utah.

*Pirata insularis.* Female ¼ inch long; male ⅙ inch. Cephalothorax brown at sides crossed by radiating lines of black and with a median forked, reddish-yellow band and a yellowish marginal stripe; abdomen blackish, with a yellow lanceolate median stripe, a yellow spot on each side of the apex, followed by several yellow chevrons or nearly straight transverse marks (Fig. 252).

Eastern and Middle States west to Utah and Colorado.

*Arctosa rubicunda.* Female about ⅖ inch long; male somewhat smaller. Cephalothorax glabrous or very nearly so; tibia of third and fourth pairs of legs with a basally stout, apically, slender, pointed bristle; anterior row of eyes wider than second row. Cephalothorax dark brown to black; abdomen gray, light in the middle with many closely placed dark dots and dashes on the sides; legs dark brown (Fig. 253).

Lives under stones in pastures and under logs in woodlands.

New England south to District of Columbia and west to Nebraska.

*Arctosa littoralis.* Female about ⅗ inch long; male the same. Cephalothorax not glabrous; anterior row of eyes shorter than second row.

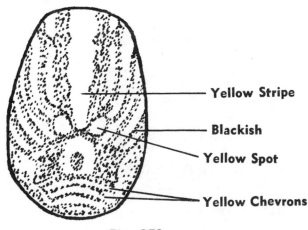

**Fig. 252**
**Pirata insularis.**

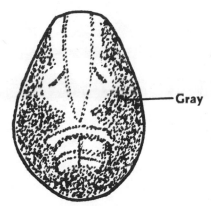

**Fig. 253**
**Arctosa rubicunda.**

This is a pale species, clothed with white, gray, and black hairs intermixed in spots and streaks and looking so much like the color of the sand over which it runs that it is not easy to see when not moving; legs spotted (Fig. 254).

Lives on beaches and sandy areas, where it sometimes digs a burrow.

A common species throughout the United States.

*Schizocosa bilineata.* Female about ¼ inch long; male about ⅕ inch. Colors yellow and light brown; cephalothorax with median light band that widens uniformly from behind toward the eyes; abdomen with a broad light band that is nearly or fully as wide as the upper surface and which encloses a lanceolate outline on the anterior half (Fig. 255); sternum of female yellow with two dark lines or rows of dark spots; tibia of first pair of legs in male with a conspicuous brush (Fig. 256) of black hairs; legs of male yellow.

In tall grass.

Maine south to Georgia and west to Kansas.

*Trabea aurantiaca.* Female ⅛ inch or a little more long; male less than ⅛ inch. Anterior row of eyes strongly procurved, anterior medians much closer to each other than to the laterals; head wider at top than at clypeus. Cephalothorax black or blackish-brown with a yellow median band, a yellow spot behind just under the front end of the abdomen, and a narrow yellow stripe on each side; abdomen brownish-orange with a yellow spot in the middle and a row of smaller spots behind; front legs dark brown, hind legs yellow with second and third pairs intermediate in color (Fig. 257).

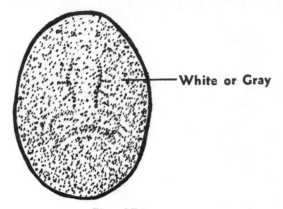

— White or Gray

**Fig. 254**
**Arctosa littoralis.**

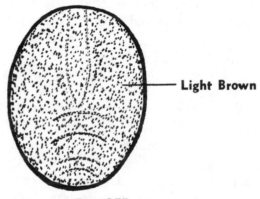

— Light Brown

**Fig. 255**
**Schizocosa bilineata.**

**Fig. 256**
**Schizocosa bilineata.**
**Tibia and Metatarsus of First Leg Showing Brush of Black Hairs.**

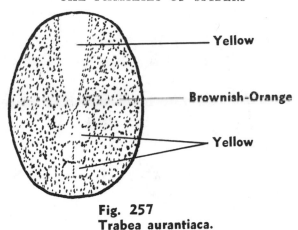

Fig. 257
Trabea aurantiaca.

Lives among dead leaves in damp woods, in swamps, and along the edge of streams.

Maine south to the District of Columbia and west to Illinois.

*Note:* The *Pardosas* are spiders of small or medium size and are true vagrants, wandering about over the ground or climbing over plants and flowers; in the fall numbers of spiderlings may be observed sailing through the air on their silken parachutes. These spiders are more gracefully built than the typical lycosids featuring a slender body supported by long thin legs that are armed with long black spines. The head is high in front; the cephalothorax is highest in the head region; the chelicerae are much smaller than in most other wolf spiders; the anterior row of eyes is shorter than the second and is procurved; the tibiae of the first pair of legs are armed with three pairs of spines.

The *Pardosas* tend to be dark in color, frequently black, with the cephalothorax usually marked by a pale longitudinal stripe continuous with a light band on the abdomen. In some of the smaller males the head and forelegs are often set with patches of white and black hairs which are presumably used during courtship.

The egg sac, which is attached to the spinnerets, is lenticular in form, usually yellowish or greenish, rarely white, sometimes of a deep blue, but changing to a dirty gray with age.

*Pardosa saxatilis.* Female about ⅕ inch long; male slightly smaller. Cephalothorax deep brown or black with a median reddish-yellow band and a narrow yellow stripe on each side; abdomen dark gray with an indistinct light lanceolate stripe on the anterior half and a series of light cross marks on the posterior half; femora of female dis-

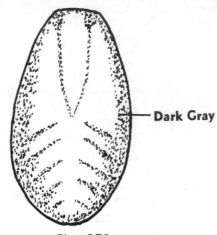

**Fig. 258**
**Pardosa saxatilis.**

tinctly marked with four rings, in the male the rings are broken into
spots except on the front legs where the femora are black (Fig. 258).

Lives in grassy fields.

Maine south to Georgia and west to the Rockies.

*Pardosa milvina.* Female about ¼ inch long; male slightly smaller.
Similar to *saxatilis* though in this species the abdomen is light in the
middle throughout its entire length, partly divided by faint cross line
of gray (Fig. 259).

Dry open woods and along the edges of ponds and streams.

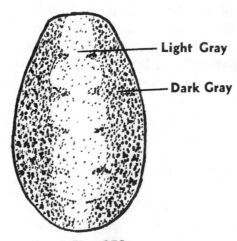

**Fig. 259**
**Pardosa milvina.**

Maine south to Georgia and west to the Rockies.

*Pardosa sternalis.* Female about ¼ inch or a little more long; male about ¼ inch. Cephalothorax black with a median brown band and a light brown band along each lateral margin; abdomen blackish with a yellow or pale brown median lanceolate stripe, with a pair of spots at the apex on the anterior half and four or five pairs of spots forming chevrons on the posterior half; in the male the cephalothorax is darker, the median band obscure, and the abdomen is entirely black above without markings.

Open meadows and the edges of streams.

Common throughout most of the United States west of the Mississippi River.

*Pardosa lapidicina.* Female about ⅓ inch long; male ¼ inch. Entire body covered with black hairs which obscure the few light markings; cephalothorax with a light median band and with a row of irregular light spots on each side; abdomen with a dark median lanceolate stripe, with a row of irregular light spots on each side on the anterior half and sometimes with a few irregular light chevrons on the posterior half (Fig. 260).

Commonly seen running over rocky borders of streams and among rocks and stones on talus slopes.

A common species in the Northern States but occurring from Maine south to Alabama and west to Nebraska and Texas.

*Pardosa xerampelina.* Female ⅓ inch long; male smaller. Cephalothorax deep brown or black with a median reddish-brown band; ab-

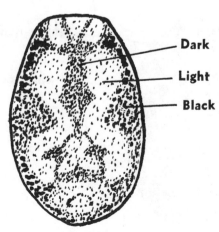

Fig. 260
Pardosa lapidicina.

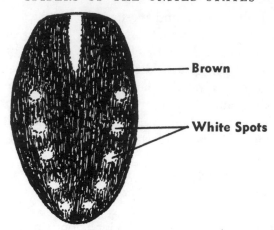

**Fig. 261**
**Pardosa groelandica.**

domen black above or nearly so with a brown lanceolate stripe on the anterior half, the stripe being joined at two points on each side near its apex by the ends of a V-shaped mark, and several more or less distinct chevrons on the posterior half.

Found essentially in mountainous regions.

A northern species occurring from New England west to Washington.

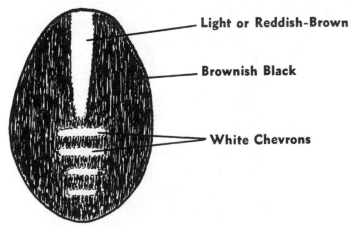

**Fig. 262**
**Pardosa modica.**

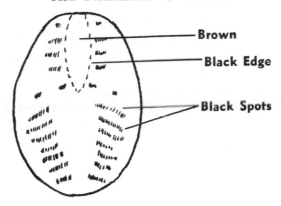

Brown

Black Edge

Black Spots

**Fig. 263**
**Pardosa emertoni.**

*Pardosa groelandica.* Female slightly more than ⁴⁄₁₀ inch long; male somewhat less. Cephalothorax black or almost black with a light brown median band from the front of which extends a horn-shaped yellow mark, both the band and the mark sometimes being absent or obscure; abdomen covered above with brown hair with bunches of white hair forming a row of white spots along each side (Fig. 261).

New England west to Washington and Colorado.

*Pardosa modica.* Female a little more than ⅓ inch long; male about ⅓ inch. Cephalothorax dark brown with a median light or reddish-brown stripe and a light stripe on each side extending under the eyes; abdomen brownish-black with a light or reddish-brown lanceolate stripe and (sometimes) four or five pairs of small spots or chevrons of white hairs on the posterior half; legs marked with longitudinal dark and light lines (Fig. 262).

A northern species occurring from New England to Oregon.

*Pardosa emertoni.* Female about ¼ inch long; male only slightly smaller. Cephalothorax yellow with two brown stripes which unite and become black between the middle eyes and a fine black line near the edge of each side; abdomen with a median light brown lanceolate stripe with a broken black edge and on each side a black band made up of spots closer toward the middle and more scattered toward the sides; legs light yellow with a few black spots near the body (Fig. 263).

A northern species occurring south to the District of Columbia.

## THE LYNX SPIDERS

*Family Oxyopidae*

The lynx spiders appear to have become specialized for living on plants since they are most generally found on vegetation or herbage and the foliage of trees and shrubs on which they run with great agility or jump from stem to stem in the manner of the jumping spiders though some prefer to sit in flowers or lie pressed against the stems of plants to await the arrival of an unfortunate insect. They hunt by day, aided by eyesight comparable to that of the wolf spiders and though they spin a dragline they make little use of silk.

The typical lynx is a well-built animal with a high, oval cephalothorax, a rounded abdomen that tapers to a point behind, and thin legs that are all about the same length and armed with long black spines (Fig. 264). The tarsi have three claws but do not have brushes of hairs. The eyes are eight in number, dark in color and unequal in size the anterior medians being very small and some of the others quite large (Fig. 265). The anterior row is strongly recurved, the posterior row procurved so that there appear to be four rows of two eyes each.

The lynxes do not carry their egg sacs about as do the wolf spiders but fasten them to a branch or leaf or hang them in a little web they spin for the purpose.

*Peucetia viridans. The Green Lynx.* Female ¾ inch long; male somewhat less. Cephalothorax highest in the region of the eyes; posterior

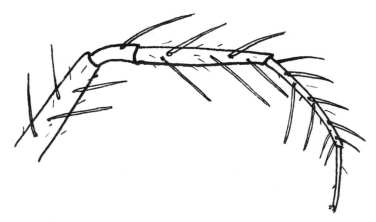

**Fig. 264**
**Leg of Oxyopes Showing Long Black Spines.**

**Fig. 265**
**Peucetia.**
**Head Showing Arrangement of Eyes.**

row of eyes slightly procurved. General color green with red spots in the eye region, on the cephalothorax, and on the abdomen, those on the abdomen being arranged in two rows and which are sometimes united to form a stripe; legs paler green to yellow with black spines and conspicuously marked with black dots, sometimes with red lines and dots (Fig. 266).

Usually found in grass.

Egg sac hemispherical in form, with small projecting tufts, and suspended among leaves and twigs.

A common species in the South where it often attracts attention because of its beautiful green color; North Carolina south to Florida and west to California.

*Oxyopes salticus. The Striped Lynx.* Female about ⅓ inch long; male slightly smaller. Posterior row of eyes strongly procurved, posterior laterals about as far from anterior laterals as from posterior medians.

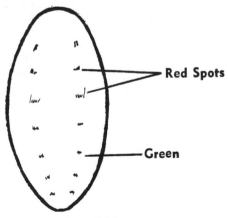

**Fig. 266**
**Peucetia viridans.**

Cephalothorax yellow with four indistinct longitudinal gray bands; a narrow black line from each anterior median eye down the clypeus and each chelicera; abdomen lighter than the cephalothorax; darker toward the anterior half, with a pointed middle spot extending as far back as the middle with narrow oblique brown marks; abdomen of male entirely gray or black with iridescent purple scales; legs pale with a narrow black line on the lower surface of the femora (Fig. 267).

Found in grass and on low bushes.

A very common species in the southern states but found as far north as New England.

*Oxyopes scalaris. The Gray Lynx.* This is a brown species uniformly clothed with gray hairs so that it appears paler than its actual color.

Widely distributed throughout the United States but especially abundant in the West where it lives on sagebrush and similar plants.

## THE JUMPING SPIDERS

*Family (Attidae) Salticidae*

The jumping spiders are of small or medium size common on plants, logs, fences, the sides of buildings and similar places where they attract our attention by their short body, stout legs, conspicuous eyes, bright colors and more particularly by their quick jumping movements. They are keen-eyed hunting spiders, pursuing their prey or springing upon it when it comes near them. They can move sidewise or backward with equal facility and can leap tremendous distances, up to forty times or more their body length, leaping from stem to stem with seeming abandon and saved from falling by the dragline which they spin wherever they go.

Because of their short body, stout legs, and distinctive eye arrangement these spiders are among the most easily recognized of all our spiders. The eyes occupy the entire length of the head, a quadrilateral area termed the ocular quadrangle, and are set in three distinct rows. The first row consists of four eyes, the two medians being very large, the second row of two small eyes, so tiny that they are often difficult to see, and the third row of two larger eyes (Fig. 268).

The cephalothorax is more or less rectangular, fairly large and wide and often quite high; the abdomen frequently oval but sometimes thick and wide or even greatly elongated and the entire body is usually thickly covered with hairs or scales that are often brightly colored.

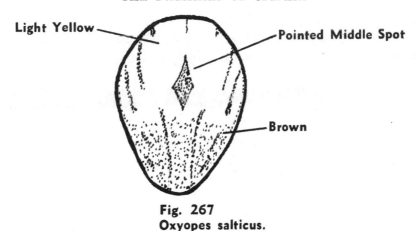

Light Yellow

Pointed Middle Spot

Brown

**Fig. 267**
**Oxyopes salticus.**

The first pair of legs is generally longer and thicker than the others and in the males are bedecked with conspicuous plumes and ornaments that are used during the courtship rituals (Fig. 269). The spiders have two tarsal claws. The sexes differ little in size but often differ greatly in color and in the form of the clothing of hairs and scales.

The jumping spiders do not spin webs but they do spin retreats in crevices, under stones on the ground, under bark, and on foliage and plants. They are sac-like in form, made of thick white slightly viscid silk of several layers, and are usually provided with two openings. Many spiders retire to these retreats at night and during cold days and also use them when molting and for passing the winter as juveniles or hibernating adults. The egg sac is usually lens-shaped and a rather

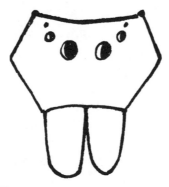

**Fig. 268**
**Face and Chelicerae of a Jumping Spider.**
**Showing Arrangement of Eyes.**

frail structure since it is made within the retreat and hence does not need to be a strong and tough affair as is the case with most spiders. The eggs and young are guarded by the female until the young disperse.

*Thiodina sylvana.* Female not quite ½ inch long; male about the same. Ocular quadrangle not more than half the length of the cephalothorax; tibiae of first pair of legs with four bulbous setae. Cephalothorax of female yellow, darkest in the eye region; eyes on black spots; a brown spot just above the anterior middle eyes; abdomen yellow with three

**Fig. 269**
**Jumping Spider Displaying Ornaments.**

longitudinal white bands, the middle sometimes not distinct, and numerous black dots; cephalothorax of male light to dark reddish-brown with a white spot between the eyes, two white lines pointing up from third and fourth legs each side and two short white lines under the dorsal eyes; abdomen light brownish-yellow to brown with two longitudinal white bands on each side of which are some scattered black dots (Fig. 270).

A southern species, occurring from the Atlantic to the Pacific.

*Ballus youngii.* Female less than ⅛ inch long; male about the same. Abdomen not much larger than cephalothorax, depressed and over-hanging the cephalothorax; tibia of first pair of legs with only one ventral and one prolateral spine. General color black, thinly covered

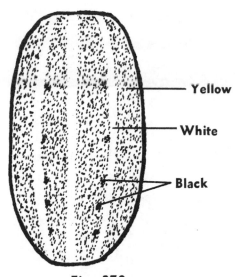

**Fig. 270**
**Thiodina sylvana.**

with short yellow hairs; ocular area black, thorax black or dark brown, abdomen black or brownish with three to five transverse yellow bands and two yellow spots on the anterior half (Fig. 271).

Usually found running over plants.

Egg sac under stones and bark.

New England west to Wisconsin.

*Synemosyna formica.* Female about ¼ inch long; male about the same.

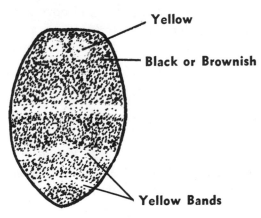

**Fig. 271**
**Ballus youngii.**

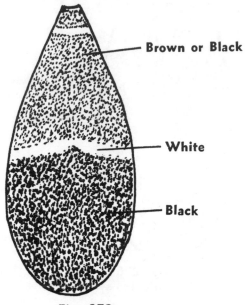

Fig. 272
Synemosyna formica.

Cephalothorax strongly constricted a short distance behind the posterior eyes, hind part narrow with parallel sides thus adding to the apparent length of the pedicel; head separated from thorax by a deep groove; abdomen with a depression near the front end; quadrangle of eyes occupies about one-third the length of the cephalothorax. Cephalothorax and anterior part of abdomen brown or black; a triangular white spot in front of the dorsal groove and one on each side widening downward under the posterior eyes; a white stripe on abdomen extending downward from the dorsal depression on each side and uniting in a large white patch underneath; posterior half of abdomen black; legs slender (Fig. 272).

The spider is amazingly ant-like in form and walks and runs in the manner of an ant; it is often mistaken for one.

On bushes and tall grass.

Maine south to Georgia and west to Wisconsin.

*Myrmarachne hentzii.* Female about ¼ inch long; male about the same. Cephalothorax long and narrow; cervical groove well marked; ocular quadrangle less than half the length of the cephalothorax; tibia and tarsus of female swollen and covered with stiff hairs. Color orange-brown or yellowish-brown with an indistinct light mark across the

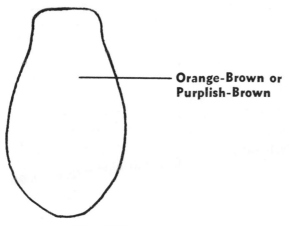

Orange-Brown or
Purplish-Brown

Fig. 273
Myrmarachne hentzii.

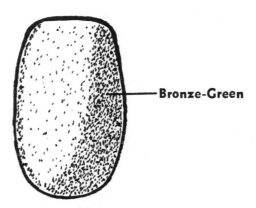

Bronze-Green

Fig. 274
Tutelina elegans.

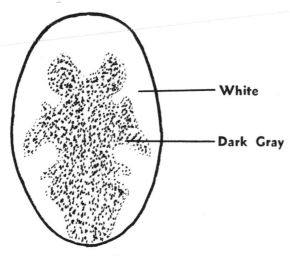

White

Dark Gray

Fig. 275
Icius hartii.

middle of the cephalothorax and another on the abdomen (Fig. 273).

Throughout the eastern half of the United States.

*Tutelina (Icius) elegans.* Female from ⅛ to ¼ inch long; male about the same. Cephalothorax not very high, slightly convex, the sides nearly parallel; ocular quadrangle occupies less than half the length of the cephalothorax; abdomen oval and twice as long as wide. Color bronze-green with brilliant iridescent scales; legs yellow with longitudinal dark stripes except femora of first pair of legs which are dark brown or black; on the head of the male are two tufts of long hairs pointing forward (Fig. 274).

Throughout the eastern half of the United States.

*Icius hartii.* Female about ¼ inch long; male about the same. Structural characters as in *elegans.* Cephalothorax brown with a covering of gray hairs; abdomen dark gray with a white border broken into bars and sometimes with a metallic iridescent sheen (Fig. 275).

Massachusetts to Nebraska.

*Talavera minuta.* Female ⅒ inch long; male ¹⁄₁₂ inch. Cephalothorax moderately high with parallel sides; ocular quadrangle occupies nearly half the length of the cephalothorax. Cephalothorax reddish-brown; eye-region black; abdomen gray with faint pale chevrons; in male abdomen black; legs white banded with black except femur of first pair of legs which is dark.

Throughout the United States.

*Neon nelli.* Female about ⅒ inch long; male about the same. Cephalothorax high, the highest part being a little behind the middle from which it curves downward to the front eyes and slopes abruptly back-

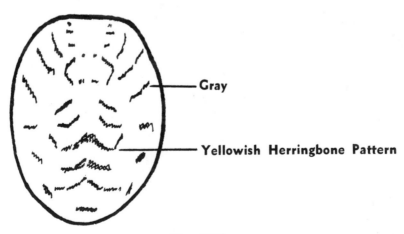

Fig. 276
Neon nelli.

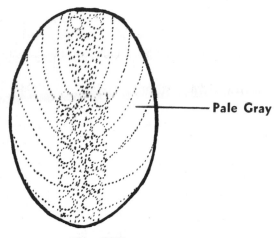

Pale Gray

**Fig. 277**
**Euophrys monadnock.**

ward; ocular quadrangle occupies more than one-half the length of the cephalothorax; anterior eyes large, prominent, close together and in a straight line, posterior laterals very large, projecting; abdomen a little longer and wider than cephalothorax. Cephalothorax brown or smoky gray, darker in the eye-region; abdomen gray with a yellowish herringbone pattern of chevrons (Fig. 276).

Common under stones and leaves.

Maine south to Georgia and west to the Pacific.

*Euophrys monadnock.* Female ⅕ inch long; male ⅙ inch. Ocular quadrangle occupies less than one-half the length of the cephalothorax; carapace less than two-thirds as wide as long; sternum oval.

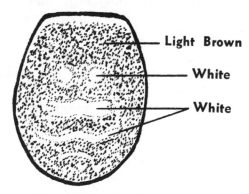

Light Brown

White

White

**Fig. 278**
**Sitticus palustris.**

Cephalothorax of female dark brown with dark radiating lines; abdomen pale gray with light chevrons on the middle and irregular oblique lines on the sides; legs tan and unmarked; male all black with legs of a contrasting black and orange-yellow (Fig. 277).

New England, the Rocky Mountain states, and Washington, Oregon and California.

*Sitticus palustris.* Female from ⅕ to ¼ inch long; male slightly smaller. Cephalothorax high, convex, somewhat wide; abdomen short and wide; ocular quadrangle occupies less than two-fifths of the length of the cephalothorax and is nearly twice as wide as long. Cephalothorax light brown in the female, dark brown in the male, with a narrow white stripe in the middle and one along each side; abdomen same color as cephalothorax with two white spots on the anterior half and a white transverse mark with several angular marks behind it on the posterior half; legs dark or light gray without any distinct markings (Fig. 278).

Lives on plants.

New England west to the Rockies.

*Salticus scenicus. The Zebra Spider.* Female about ¼ inch long; male about the same or slightly smaller. Cephalothorax much longer than wide; abdomen long and narrow with sides nearly parallel; ocular quadrangle occupies much less than one-half the length of the cephalothorax; anterior eyes unequal in size. General color gray with white markings but sometimes brown to reddish scales are mixed in with the gray; front of head around and above the eyes white; a white band across the anterior end of the abdomen and two or three oblique white bands on the sides; legs gray with white rings not distinctly marked (Fig. 279).

A very common spider found on houses and fences; sometimes wanders indoors.

Throughout the United States.

*Hyctia pikei.* Female ¼ to ⅓ inch long; male about the same or slightly smaller. Abdomen twice as long as the cephalothorax; tibia of first pair of legs with four pairs of spines. General color gray with brown markings; abdomen of male with a wide black stripe with four notches on each side on the middle and a white stripe on each side, abdomen of female with a stripe dark brown and less definite and broken into spots; front legs of both sexes as long as abdomen, brown, with middle segments thickened, other legs pale and slender (Fig. 280). The elongated shape of this spider distinguishes it from all the other common jumping spiders; the position of the legs, two pairs

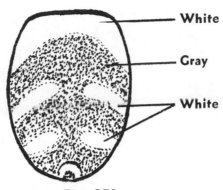

Fig. 279
Salticus scenicus.

pointing forward and two backward increases its long appearance.
Throughout the eastern half of the United States.

*Marpissa undata.* Female about ½ inch long; male somewhat
smaller. Cephalothorax about four-fifths as wide as long with the sides
curved outward; cephalothorax and abdomen both flattened and
hairy; rear eyes far from lateral edges; first pair of legs somewhat
stouter than second pair with three pairs of spines beneath the tibia.

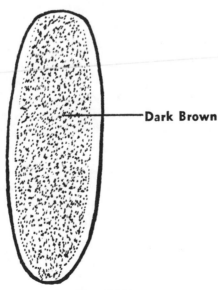

Fig. 280
Hyctia pikei.

General color gray, body being covered with long, white, gray, and dull reddish hairs; cephalothorax with a dark brown band along the edge on each side; abdomen with a broad pale yellow median stripe, the posterior half notched at the sides, and containing within it a darker line; legs darker at the ends of the segments and light in the middle (Fig. 281).

Common on fences, under loose bark, and on the outside of buildings.

Eastern half of the United States west to Utah.

*Admestina tibialis.* Female about ⅙ inch long; male about the same. Cephalothorax, long, narrow in front and black or brown; abdomen pale and marked with one or two black bands which are often notched; first pair of legs brown, the others pale, spotted or lined in black.

Throughout the eastern half of the United States west to Wisconsin and Texas.

*Wala palmarum.* Female about ⅕ inch long; male about the same. Cephalothorax nearly flat, longer than wide; ocular quadrangle occupies less than one-half the length of the cephalothorax; anterior eyes in a straight or slightly procurved line; abdomen long and narrow; first pair of legs in male much longer than the others. Cephalothorax of female reddish, eyes on dark spots; abdomen light with large triangular spots in the middle and small dark spots at the sides; legs white; male reddish with a broad white band on the sides extending the entire length of the body; front legs dark, others white (Fig. 282).

Common on trees and low bushes.

Throughout the eastern half of the United States.

*Note:* The following spiders of the genus *Phidippus* are the heaviest and hairiest of our jumping spiders. They are above medium size with a high, heavy and convex cephalothorax and with the first pair of legs heavy and hairy and often fringed. Posterior row of eyes about one and a quarter times as wide as the first row. Males often with tufts of hairs about the eyes.

*Phidippus audax.* Female from ⅓ to ½ inch long; male slightly smaller. Cephalothorax and abdomen black with many long white hairs; abdomen with a white basal band with several white (though sometimes yellow or orange) spots behind the largest of which is triangular in outline; legs with segments grayish in the middle and black toward the ends (Fig. 283).

An extremely common spider found living under stones and boards on the ground or running about on tree trunks.

Eastern half of the United States west to the Rockies.

*Phidippus variegatus.* Female about ½ inch long; male slightly

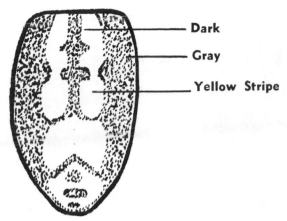

Fig. 281
Marpissa undata.

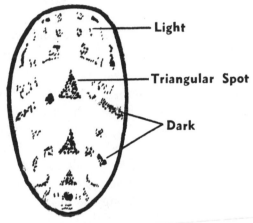

Fig. 282
Wala palmarum.

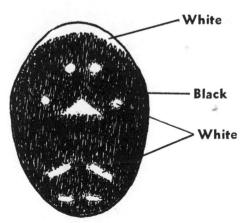

Fig. 283
Phidippus audax.

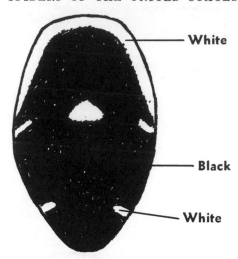

Fig. 284
Phidippus variegatus.

smaller. Cephalothorax black with two white bands on the sides; abdomen black with a white basal band, a large central white triangular spot, and farther back on the sides two pairs of white bars; tibia of first pair of legs heavily fringed (Fig. 284).

A southern species found throughout the Gulf States.

*Phidippus whitmanii.* Female about ½ inch long; male slightly smaller. Cephalothorax and abdomen of male red; cephalothorax with a black hairless region crossing the head in front of the small eyes and abdomen with an indistinct basal yellow stripe; cephalothorax and abdo-

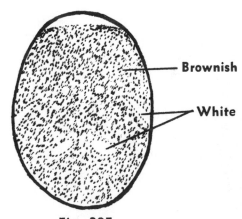

Fig. 285
Phidippus whitmanii.

men of female duller to brownish with several pairs of indistinct white spots on abdomen (Fig. 285).

Lives on bushes and herbaceous plants.

A northern species occurring from New England west to Wisconsin.

*Phidippus clarus.* Female from ⅓ to ½ inch long; male somewhat smaller. Cephalothorax and abdomen of female red, abdomen with longitudinal black stripes spotted with white, a basal white band, and oblique white bands on the sides; cephalothorax of male black, abdomen red with a central longitudinal black band, the margins notched by three pairs of red or white spots, a basal white band, and oblique white bands on the sides.

Throughout the United States.

*Phidippus insolens.* Female about ½ inch long; male slightly smaller. Cephalothorax of female red on upper surface, black at the sides, abdomen sometimes red on the upper surface, sometimes with a small black V above the spinnerets, a faint white or yellowish basal band and a white or yellowish diagonal on each side; cephalothorax of male black covered with inconspicuous brownish hairs; abdomen black with red bands and spots or uniformly red.

Throughout the southern states.

*Phidippus purpuratus.* Female about ½ inch long; male slightly smaller. Cephalothorax densely covered with gray hairs; abdomen light gray with a broad dark middle band marked with four pairs of white spots (Fig. 286).

Usually found under stones and other objects lying on the ground.

Maine west to Missouri and Texas.

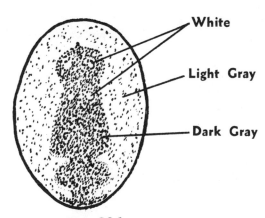

**Fig. 286**
**Phidippus purpuratus.**

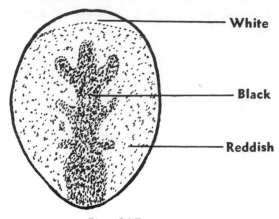

**Fig. 287**
**Phidippus rimator.**

*Phidippus rimator.* Female about ⅜ inch long; male somewhat smaller.
Female yellowish-orange to brown with black and white markings;
cephalothorax of male black, abdomen with broad black middle band,
a white basal band, and reddish lateral stripes (Fig. 287).

Found on bushes and in tall grass.

Throughout the United States.

*Dendryphantes (Paraphidippus) marginatus.* Female ⅓ inch long;
male ¼ inch. Cephalothorax high, convex, highest at the third row
of eyes; ocular quadrangle occupies two-fifths the length of the ceph-

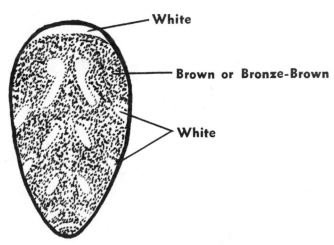

**Fig. 288**
**Dendryphantes marginatus.**

alothorax; anterior eyes large, second row halfway between the other rows; first pair of legs in male fringed. Female brown or bronze-brown, abdomen with a basal white band and several pairs of somewhat oblique white spots; male yellowish-brown or bronze-brown, cephalothorax with a white band on each side, abdomen with an encircling white band (Fig. 288).

Common on shrubbery and in tall grass.

Throughout the United States.

*Dendryphantes (Paraphidippus capitatus) aestivalis.* Female from ⅕ to ¼ inch long; male smaller. Female in two varieties: light variety with light parts white or light yellow and dark parts dark brown covered with hairs and scales. Cephalothorax dark brown with few scales so that the dark color shows between them; abdomen lighter than cephalothorax with four pairs of purplish-brown spots, the second pair the largest; legs light yellow indistinctly ringed with brown at the base and, near the tip of each segment, with greenish-white hairs. Dark variety covered with longer hairs and scales, the dark spots on abdomen larger, and the legs more distinctly ringed. Cephalothorax of males dark brown with a white stripe on each side under the eyes; front of head white and covered with long white hairs; abdomen white in front and around the sides, the middle dark brown, often notched at the sides, and with a few yellow and greenish scales; legs ringed as in female (Fig. 289).

Common on bushes and small trees.

Throughout the United States.

*Sassacus papenhoei.* Female a little more than ⅕ inch long; male a little less. Cephalothorax short and thick, flat in the first two-thirds; ocular quadrangle wider behind than in front and occupies one-half the length of the cephalothorax; small eyes a little closer to the anterior row than posterior; tibia of first pair of legs with two or three pairs of spines. Dark in color and covered with iridescent scales; cephalothorax with a white marginal stripe on each side and abdomen with a white basal band which is continued along each side; legs reddish with last two segments white with black rings at the distal end of each (Fig. 290).

Ohio and Tennessee west to the Pacific.

*Agassa cyanea.* Female a little less than ⅕ inch long; male slightly smaller. Cephalothorax thick, about as wide as long, flat above, and hollowed behind; abdomen oval, short, and truncate in front; ocular quadrangle occupies two-thirds of the length of the cephalothorax; second row of eyes twice as far from the posterior row as from the

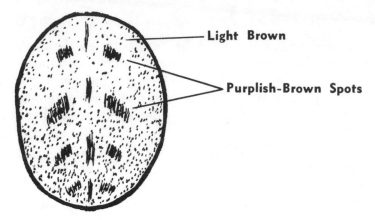

Light Brown

Purplish-Brown Spots

Fig. 289
Dendryphantes aestivalis.

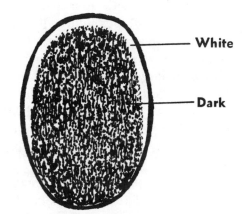

White

Dark

Fig. 290
Sassacus papenhoei.

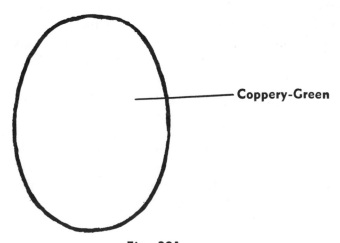

Coppery-Green

Fig. 291
Agassa cyanea.

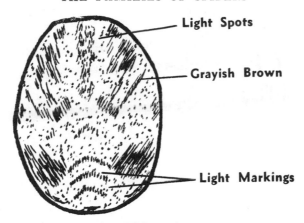

Light Spots

Grayish Brown

Light Markings

**Fig. 292**
**Habrocestum pulex.**

anterior. Entire body covered with iridescent scales that give it a coppery-green color (Fig. 291).

Throughout the United States east of the Rocky Mountains.

*Habrocestum pulex.* Female a little more than ⅙ inch long; male about the same. Cephalothorax high, cephalic part convex, thoracic part sloping; ocular quadrangle occupies less than one-half the length of the cephalothorax; anterior row of eyes wider than posterior; abdomen elongate oval. Cephalothorax of female grayish-brown with several irregular light spots on the basal half and a transverse light band nearly the whole width of the abdomen just behind the middle with several smaller light markings towards the end; cephalothorax of male reddish or orange-brown to yellow with cephalic part black; abdomen darker than in female but similarly marked; legs light and dark spotted, the contrast stronger in the male (Fig. 292).

Found in open places where it may be seen hopping about on stones and dry leaves.

Throughout the eastern half of the country, from Maine south to Georgia and west to Nebraska and Louisiana.

*Phlegra leopardus. The Leopard Spider.* Female about ¼ inch long; male a little less. Cephalothorax long and narrow, widest behind the middle; abdomen elongate oval; ocular quadrangle occupies only about one-third the length of the cephalothorax; anterior row of eyes recurved; tibia of first pair of legs with three pairs of ventral spines. Cephalothorax with two white stripes, abdomen with three, on a dark or brown ground (Fig. 293).

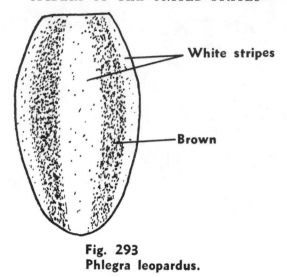

**Fig. 293**
**Phlegra leopardus.**

Throughout the eastern half of the United States.
*Note:* The spiders of *Pellenes (Habronattus)* have a high convex ceph-alothorax which is a little longer than wide. The ocular quadrangle is wider than long and as a rule wider behind than in front; the second row of eyes is about midway between the first and third; the third pair of legs is longer than the first pair; and the males usually have some peculiar modification of form, color, or ornament on the first and third pairs of legs which are used to attract the female during courtship (Fig. 293A).
*Pellenes (Habronattus) agilis.* Female ¼ inch long; male ⅕ inch. Cephalothorax of male covered with short black hairs and some of

**Fig. 293A**
**Leg of Pellenes Showing Ornaments.**

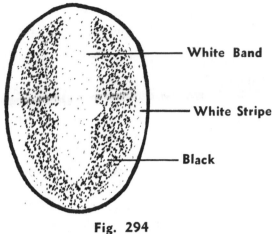

**White Band**

**White Stripe**

**Black**

**Fig. 294**
**Pellenes agilis.**

a yellowish-brown color, with a short median white stripe and three black and four white longitudinal stripes; abdomen black with a white median notched band, two black bands and two white stripes; first pair of legs heavily fringed with white; cephalothorax of female with gray hairs instead of black and markings less distinct; abdomen with median band broken into several spots or pairs of spots (Fig. 294).

Maine south to Georgia and west to the Rockies.

*Pellenes (Habronattus) borealis.* Female ¼ inch long; male slightly more than one-fifth inch. Cephalothorax of male all black; abdomen black with a white basal band, a white encircling band which sends up two bars on each side, the anterior pair continued in a transverse band, and a central white spot with two white dots behind it on the posterior half; cephalothorax and abdomen of female dark gray, cephalothorax with light gray dorsal and marginal bands, the abdomen with light gray basal and transverse bands, two fawn dots behind the transverse band, and still farther back four chevrons and two dots of the same color (Fig. 295).

Maine west to Washington and south to North Carolina.

*Pellenes (Habronattus) coronatus.* Female ⅕ inch long; male ⅙ inch. Cephalic part of male with red or orange hairs, thoracic part dark to pale with a pair of white longitudinal lines extending back from the posterior eyes; abdomen black or brown with a white basal band, a transverse stripe near the middle, a central spot behind it followed by a pair of spots above the spinnerets; female yellowish with whitish bands less distinct than those of male; femur of third pair of legs rounded into a shiny boss at distal end and patella with a short spur at its end.

A southern species but found as far north as New England; west to Texas and Colorado.

*Pellenes (Habronattus) hoyi.* Female ¼ inch long; male ⅕ inch. Cephalothorax of male with upper part bright yellowish-red with a snowy band above the front eyes and which curves back to the second row of eyes; abdomen light golden on the upper surface with an encircling white band bordered with red around the base and front sides, and with black toward the spinnerets; cephalothorax of female with a mixture of orange, black, and white hairs, sides lighter than the back; abdomen with a pale golden area down the middle, sometimes marked with fine white chevrons, and a black, or black mixed with red, band on each side.

Throughout the United States.

*Pellenes (Hebronattus) peregrinus.* Female ¼ inch long; male ⅕ inch. Cephalothorax with a white stripe on each side which extends from the anterior lateral eyes backward and then curves inward on the anterior half of the thorax and then outward on the posterior half; abdomen with three white longitudinal stripes; first pair of legs in males fringed, patella of third legs wide, flat with a dark spot in the middle of the front side (Fig. 296).

Eastern United States from Maine to Florida.

*Pellenes (Habronattus) splendens.* Female about ¼ inch long; the male a little smaller. Cephalothorax of female covered with brown scales

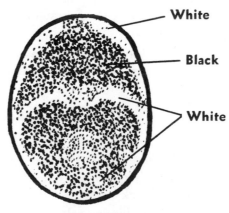

**Fig. 295**
**Pellenes borealis.**

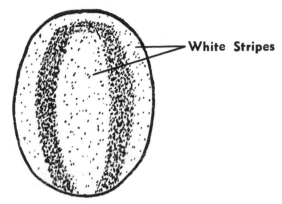

Fig. 296
Pellenes peregrinus.

mixed with black hairs with a light band across the middle just behind the dorsal eyes, the band curving behind the eyes and extending forward in the middle; abdomen velvety black with a white band at the base, one on each side, and one in the middle; cephalothorax of male covered with iridescent scales, with blue, green, and purple reflections; abdomen with bright red or pinkish red shiny scales mixed with fine black hairs (Fig. 297).

Throughout the United States.

*Plexippus paykulli.* Female from ³⁄₁₀ to little more than ⁴⁄₁₀ inch long; male a little less. Cephalothorax high, convex, with rounded sides; ocular quadrangle occupies about one-third the length of the cephalothorax; tibia of first pair of legs with three pairs of spines. Cephalic

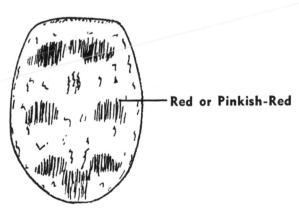

Fig. 297
Pellenes splendens.

part of cephalothorax black, thoracic part brown with a light median stripe; abdomen black with a yellow median line and white lateral lines, the median line divided by a dark line on the anterior half of the abdomen and with indistinct dark chevrons and a pair of transverse white bars on the posterior half (Fig. 298).

A southern species found from Georgia and Florida west to Texas.

*Metacyrba taeniola.* Female a little more than ¼ inch long; male a little less than ⅕ inch. Cephalothorax low, flat, narrow in front and in back; ocular quadrangle wider than long, front middle eyes large, close together, lateral eyes half as large and somewhat separated from them; first pair of legs twice as thick as the others with femora flattened. Cephalothorax black or mahogany brown, smooth, and without markings; abdomen dark gray with two white or whitish-yellow lines more or less broken into spots or bars (Fig. 299).

Throughout the eastern half of the United States and west to Oklahoma and California.

*Maevia vittata.* Female about ⅓ inch long; male slightly smaller. Cephalothorax rather high and slightly rounded sides; ocular quadrangle slightly wider in front than behind and occupies less than one-half the length of the cephalothorax; anterior eyes in a straight or slightly recurved line, second row nearly midway between first and third rows; legs slender and unusually long for this family, the fourth pair longest in the female, the first and fourth pairs of equal length in the male. Cephalothorax light brown with three more or less distinct longitudinal fine lines, ocular quadrangle black or dark brown; abdomen with gray scales mixed with black hairs on the sides and middle with two longitudinal red or light red bands with indistinct chevrons of the same color on the posterior half; legs yellow or greenish white. Male of two varieties. The typical male resembles the female except that the red bands on the abdomen are broken into two rows of spots which are connected with the chevrons. In the other variety the male is black on both the cephalothorax and abdomen though there is a pale spot in the center of the thorax which is divided by a longitudinal black line (Fig. 300).

Maine south to Georgia and west to Nebraska and Oklahoma.

*Onondaga lineata.* Female about ⅕ inch; male slightly less. Cephalothorax low, nearly flat, with a transverse groove behind the dorsal eyes; ocular quadrangle occupies less than half the length of the cephalothorax and is somewhat wider behind than in front; second row of eyes a little nearer the third than the first; tibia of first pair of legs thickened with four pairs of ventral spines. Cephalothorax light brown; ocular quadrangle black; abdomen with four white lines;

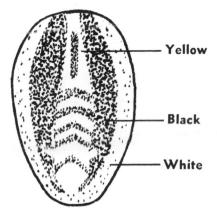

Fig. 298
Plexippus paykulli.

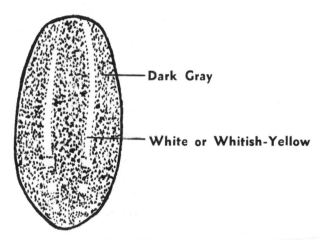

Fig. 299
Metacyrba taeniola.

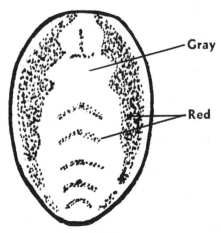

Fig. 300
Maevia vittata.

legs of female brown, of male yellow, except for the tibia of the first pair which is dark (Fig. 301).

Maine south to Florida and west to Wisconsin.

*Zygoballus bettini.* Female about ¼ inch long; male slightly less. Cephalothorax high and wide in the middle, sloping down steeply from the posterior eyes under the front of the abdomen, ocular quadrangle occupies more than half the length of the cephalothorax; first

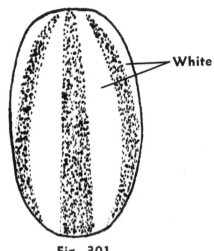

**Fig. 301**
**Onondaga lineata.**

pair of legs much stouter than the others; chelicerae of males greatly enlarged, with a hammer-like process on lower surface. Cephalothorax of female bronze-brown; abdomen light brown with a white basal transverse band, two angular white bands on the anterior part and several whitish chevrons on the posterior part; legs pale except the dark femora of the first pair and dark spots on the ends of the segments of the fourth pair; cephalothorax of male darker than that of female with red and green iridescence on the cephalic part; abdomen brown with shining scales and two pairs of white spots parallel to each other; legs little darker than those of female with the spots on the fourth pair of legs wanting (Fig. 302).

A common species from Maine to Florida and west to Nebraska and Texas.

*Zygoballus nervosus.* Female and male about same size as *bettini.*

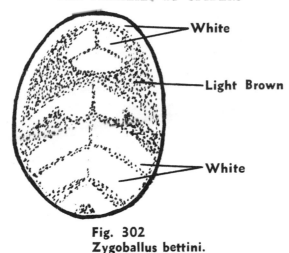

**Fig. 302**
**Zygoballus bettini.**

Cephalothorax brown, thinly covered with whitish scales; abdomen of male brown with a very bright white basal band extending two-thirds of the way along the sides, a nearly longitudinal white bar edged with black on each side of the posterior end and a white spot at the spinnerets; abdomen of female lighter brown with two short curved bands just back of the basal band, followed by two large white spots with black spots behind them and farther back a series of indistinct whitish chevrons.

Maine west to Illinois and south to Virginia.

*Zygoballus sexpunctatus.* Female about ⅛ inch long; male slightly less. Similar to *bettini* except that the male has a large white spot in

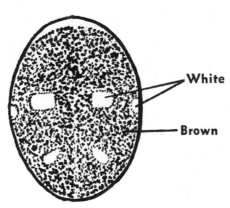

**Fig. 303**
**Zygoballus sexpunctatus.**

the middle of the cephalothorax and with six white spots on the abdomen though the spots may be absent (Fig. 303).

A southern species found from New Jersey south to Florida and west to Texas.

*Peckhamia picata.* Female about ⅛ inch or slightly more; male somewhat less. Cephalothorax convex above in ocular region, thoracic part short, with a conspicuous constriction behind the rear eyes; ocular quadrangle occupies more than one-half the length of the cephalothorax; ocular area black with violet reflections; thorax reddish-brown with a pair of white spots behind the posterior lateral eyes; abdomen reddish-brown on anterior half, black on posterior half with a white band on each side in the constriction; upper surface in both sexes covered with a thick shiny scutum. Ant-like in form with the pedicel of the abdomen visible from above (Fig. 304).

Maine south to Alabama and west to Nebraska.

*Peckhamia scorpiona.* Female about ⅒ inch long; male somewhat less. Cephalothorax of female brownish-white, eyes on black spots; abdomen pale with two short, curved dark bands near the spinnerets; cephalothorax of male brown; abdomen brown in anterior part, encircled by a white line in front of the middle, blackish behind.

Throughout the United States.

*Peckhamia americana.* Female about ⅕ inch long; male somewhat less. Somewhat similar to *picata* but lighter in color.

A southern species found in the Gulf States and in the Southwest.

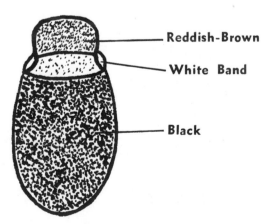

Reddish-Brown

White Band

Black

**Fig. 304**
**Peckhamia picata.**

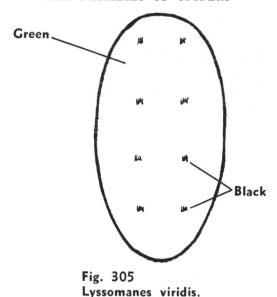

**Fig. 305**
**Lyssomanes viridis.**

*Note:* Though the species of *Metphidippus* are among the more common of the jumping spiders, they show so much variation in pattern and in degree of pigmentation that they are somewhat difficult to identify except by the expert araneologist. *Metaphidippus protervus,* found throughout the United States, has four pairs of black to reddish spots on the abdomen; *Metaphidippus insignis,* found from New England west to the Mississippi, has five pairs of black spots on the abdomen though the first pair is often indistinct; and *Metaphidippus canadensis,* found from New England south to the mountains of North Carolina and Tennessee and westward to the Mississippi, has a series of very narrow light chevrons on the abdomen.

## THE LYSSOMANIDS

*Family Lyssomanidae*

The spiders of this family have their eyes in four rows, each row consisting of two eyes (Fig. 7). We have only one species in the United States.

*Lyssomanes viridis.* Female ⅓ inch long; male ¼ inch. Cephalothorax narrow in front; abdomen narrower than thorax and more than twice as long as wide; legs long and slender, first pair longest. Color a bright green with black around the second, third, and fourth rows of eyes; abdomen sometimes with four pairs of small black dots (Fig. 305).

Lives on low bushes.

A southern species found from North Carolina south to Florida and west to Texas.

# 4
# COLLECTING AND
# PRESERVING SPIDERS

For those who may want to collect and preserve spiders the following notes might be helpful. Spiders may be picked up with the fingers or with a pair of forceps or with a camel's hair brush moistened with alcohol for very small species and placed in a collecting jar of alcohol. A cyanide tube (which may be purchased from a biological supply house) or a dry vial may also be used, the tube or vial being placed over the spider and a sheet of paper passed between the mouth of the tube or vial and the object on which the spider is resting to prevent the spider from escaping as the tube or vial is raised. A dry vial has the advantage of keeping the spider alive for a while so that the collector may examine it before transferring it to the collecting bottle. Bear in mind that a dead spider will shrivel up rather quickly so it is advisable to place a dead spider in alcohol as soon as possible.

One of the easiest ways of getting a large number of spiders at one time is to pass an insect sweeping net (which can be purchased from a biological supply house or made at home) through tall grass and weeds and picking the spiders from among the insects, leaves, flowers, and debris that will thus be collected. Beating bushes and shaking small trees will usually produce a number of spiders after first placing a light-colored cloth on the ground to show those that fall. The litter from the woodland floor is also usually quite productive.

It should be gathered up and placed in the center of a dull-colored piece of cloth (white cloth is apt to be too dazzling in the sun) and then removed bit by bit, the spiders being picked up as they scurry around.

Most spiders will be found on plants, but many will be found on the ground, beneath stones, sticks, logs and other objects, in woodland litter, in houses, barns, and outbuildings as well as on fences. Most of us are likely to look for spiders during the daytime, but some species, especially many of the wolf spiders, are perhaps better collected at night with the aid of an electric torch which can be carried in the hand or worn on the forehead like a miner's lamp. And it must be remembered that many torpid spiders can be collected during the winter. A bag can be filled with forest litter and the material carried home and sifted over a table, the spiders being picked up after they have warmed up and become active.

If spiders are desired to be kept alive for study or for any other purpose they may safely be kept in an ordinary tumbler, except for the larger species which may be kept in a mason jar. The mouth of the tumbler or jar should be plugged with a wad of cotton wrapped and tied in a piece of cheesecloth. This will not only allow the air to circulate but will also prevent the cotton from being pulled apart and the spider and its insect food from escaping. Spiders can go for rather lengthy periods without food but a drop or two of water should be placed in the tumbler or jar each day.

Spiders may be preserved in vials containing undiluted alcohol or various dilutions down to 70%. Colors unfortunately are not too well preserved in alcohol but some success may be obtained by adding a little formalin. Each vial containing a spider should have the name of the spider, its sex, and the place and date where it was collected as well as the collector's name.

# GLOSSARY

ABDOMEN. The second or posterior region of the two main divisions into which a spider's body is divided.

ACCESSORY CLAWS. The serrated bristles on the tip of the tarsus in some spiders.

ANAL TUBERCLE. A small rounded projection at the posterior end bearing the anal opening.

ANNULUS. A pigment ring on an appendage.

ANTERIOR. Toward the front.

ANTERIOR LATERAL EYES. The eye at each end of the first row.

ANTERIOR MEDIAN EYES. The two intermediate eyes of the first row.

APPENDAGE. A structure extending from the body as a leg, etc.

ARACHNIDA. A division, or class, of the air-breathing arthropods that includes the spiders, scorpions, mites, harvestmen, etc.

ARACHNOLOGIST. A student of the arachnids or one who studies the arachnids.

ARANEAE. The ordinal name of all spiders.

ARANEOLOGY. The branch of zoology that treats only of spiders.

ARTHROPOD. A jointed-legged animal such as a crustacean, insect, spider, scorpion, centipede, millipede, etc.; a member of the phylum Arthropoda.

ATTACHMENT DISC. The series of tiny lines that serve to anchor the dragline of a spider.

AUTOPHAGY. The eating of an appendage shed from the body.

AUTOSPASY. The loss of an appendage by breaking it at a locus of weakness when subjected to an outside force.

BALLOONING. Flying through the air on strands of silk spun by spiders.

251

BOOK LUNGS. Sacs filled with air and provided with leaf-like folds that afford maximum surface area for aeration.

BOSS. A smooth prominence at the outer angle of the base of the chelicera in some spiders.

BRIDGE LINE. A silken strand spun by the spider and carried by air currents until it adheres to a distant object; the spider then pulls the strand taut and fastens it where it is standing, the strand then becoming a bridge on which the spider can move and from which it can begin its web-spinning operation.

BRISTLE. A long thin extension of the cuticula; a short, stiff, coarse hair.

CALAMISTRUM. A row of curved hairs on the hind metatarsus of some spiders used to comb the silk from the cribellum.

CARAPACE. The hard covering forming the dorsal wall of the cephalothorax.

CARINA. A keel on the clypeus or chelicerae in some spiders.

CARNIVOROUS. Eating or living on other animals.

CAUDAL. Toward the posterior or rear end.

CEPHALOTHORAX. The anterior or first of the two main divisions into which a spider's body is divided.

CERVICAL GROOVE. The furrow or groove which extends forward and toward the sides from the middle of the cephalothorax. It marks the boundary between the head and thorax.

CHELICERAE. The pincer-like first pair of appendages; they consist of a stout basal segment and terminal fang.

CHITIN. An organic substance in the cuticula that gives it hardness or firmness.

CLAW. A strong curved process at the distal end of a leg.

CLAW TUFTS. The bunches of hairs below the paired claws at the tip of the tarsi of many spiders.

CLYPEUS. The space between the anterior row of eyes and the anterior edge of the carapace.

COLULUS. The slender and pointed appendage located between and in front of the anterior spinnerets of some spiders.

COURTSHIP. The behavior or ritual engaged in by spiders antecedent to mating.

COXA. The segment of the leg nearest the body.

CRIBELLUM. A sieve-like, transverse plate located in front of the spinnerets in some spiders and used as a spinning organ.

CUTICLE. The hard outer covering of an arthropod.

DIAD. A pair, as of two eyes placed close together.

DIMORPHISM. Two individuals of the same species that differ in size, structure, form, color, etc.

DORSAL. Pertaining to the back as opposed to the ventral or belly of a bilaterally symmetrical animal.

DORSAL FURROW OR GROOVE. A conspicuous depression or pigmented line behind the cervical groove in many spiders.

DORSUM. The upper surface.

DRAGLINE. A thread of silk spun by spiders as they move from place to place which marks their course.

ECDYSIS. The process of casting the skin; molting.

EGG SAC. Generally the silk with which the female spider covers her mass of eggs and molds into a shape or form characteristic of the species.

ENDITE. The plate borne by the coxa of the pedipalps of most spiders and used to crush the prey; the maxilla.

EPIGASTRIC FURROW. A groove or furrow separating the region of the book lungs from the more posterior part of the abdomen.

EPIGYNUM. A more or less complicated apparatus for storing the spermatozoa, immediately in front of the opening of the internal reproductive organs of female spiders.

EYE-SPACE. The part of the head between the rows of eyes.

FANG. The claw-like distal segment of the chelicera.

FEMUR. The third segment of the pedipalps and legs counting from the proximal end or the point of attachment.

FOLIUM. A pigmented design or pattern on the upper surface of the abdomen.

GENITALIA. The reproductive organs such as the palp of the male and the epigynum of the female.

GENITAL OPENING OR PORE. The opening on the lower surface of the abdomen through which sperms and eggs emerge.

GENUS. The taxonomic subdivision of a family.

HACKLED BAND. The threads spun by the cribellum and combed by the calamistrum; characteristic of the cribellate spiders.

HEAD. The part of the cephalothorax which bears the eyes and the so-called mouth-parts.

HETEROGENEOUS EYES. Eyes not all of the same dark or light color.

HOMOGENEOUS EYES. Eyes all of the same dark or light color.

INTEGUMENT. The outer covering or cuticle of the spider.

LABIUM. The lower lip forming the floor of the mouth cavity.

LATERAL CONDYLE. A smooth prominence at the base of the chelicera in many spiders.

LATERIGRADE. A sidewise form of locomotion characteristic of the crab spiders and their allies; the manner in which the legs are turned so that the morphologically dorsal surface is posterior.

LORUM. The set of plates on the upper surface of the pedicel.

LUNG-SLITS. The external openings of the book-lungs.

MAXILLA. Same as endite.

MEDIAN OCULAR AREA. The space limited by the four median eyes.

METATARSUS. The sixth segment of the leg, counting from the point of attachment.

MIMICRY. The resemblance of a spider to another animal or some other object.

MOLTING. The periodic process of shedding the cuticle or integument accompanied by the formation of a new one.

OCULAR QUADRANGLE. The space occupied by the eyes of the jumping spiders.

OCULAR TUBERCLE. The elevated part of the head, in some spiders, on which the eyes are situated.

PALP OR PALPUS. The segmented appendage of the pedipalp, exclusive of the coxa and endite; it is simple in the female but in the male it is modified for sperm transfer.

PATELLA. The fourth segment of the leg counting from the point of attachment.

PEDICEL. The small stalk which connects the abdomen with the cephalothorax.

PEDIPALPS. The second pair of appendages of the head.

POISON GLAND. The gland which secretes the venom of the spider.

POSTERIOR LATERAL EYES. The eye at each end of the second row.

POSTERIOR MEDIAN EYES. The two intermediate eyes of the second row.

PROCURVED EYE ROW. When the lateral eyes are farther forward than the median eyes.

PROLATERAL SURFACE. The surface of the leg nearest the anterior end of the spider's body.

PROMARGIN. The margin of the fang furrow away from the endite.

PROMARGINAL TEETH. The teeth on the anterior or upper side of the groove in which the fang lies when not in use.

RADIAL FURROW. A depression or pigmented line sometimes present behind the cervical groove.

RECURVED EYE ROW. When the lateral eyes are farther back than the median eyes.

REGENERATION. Replacement by growth of an appendage lost or missing.

RETROMARGIN. The margin of the fang furrow nearer the endite.

RETROMARGINAL TEETH. The teeth on the posterior or lower side of the groove in which the fang lies when not in use.

SCALE. A flattened, modified seta.

SCOPULA. A brush of hairs on the lower surface of the tarsus and meta-tarsus in some spiders.

SCUTUM. A sclerotized plate sometimes occurring on the abdomen.

SEGMENT. A ring, section, or subdivision of the body or of an appendage.

SERRATED BRISTLE. A type of bristle with teeth along one side and usually slightly curved.

SERRULA. A finely toothed keel on the distal margin of the endite.

SETA. A slender, hairlike or spinelike appendage of the body.

SEXUAL DIMORPHISM. The two sexes of a given species that differ in size, structure, form, color, etc.

SPERM INDUCTION. The process by which the spermatozoa are transferred from the genital orifice beneath the base of the abdomen into the receptacle of the male palpus.

SPIDERLING. A tiny, immature spider, usually the form which has just emerged from the egg sac.

SPINNERETS. The fingerlike abdominal appendages through which the silk is spun.

SPIRACLE. The external opening of the trachea or air-tube.

STABILIMENTUM. A heavy band of silk placed in the web by some orb-weaving spiders.

STERNUM. The sclerite forming the ventral wall of the cephalothorax and lying between the coxae.

STRIDULATING ORGAN. An area with numerous parallel striae on the lateral surface of the chelicerae of some spiders or on the posterior part of the carapace in others.

TARSUS. The last segment of the leg or palp.

TERGUM. The dorsal portion of the exoskeleton of any body segment.

TENENT HAIRS. Hairs dilated at the extremity and which serve to help the spider to cling to a smooth surface.

TERMINAL TENENT HAIRS. A bunch of tenent hairs at the tip of the tarsus just below the claws.

THORACIC FURROW OR GROOVE. Same as dorsal furrow or groove.

THORAX. The second body region fused with the head to form the cephalothorax.

TIBIA. The fifth segment of the leg or palp counting from the point of attachment.

TRACHEAE. Tubes through which air is carried around inside the body of the spider and which open to the outside by means of the spiracles.

TRICHOBOTHRIUM. A very fine hair extending out at right angles from the surface of the leg.

TROCHANTER. The second segment of the leg or palp counting from the point of attachment.

TUBERCLE. A low, usually rounded, process.

VENOM. The poison secreted by the poison gland.

VENTRAL. The lower surface of the body, away from the back.

VISCID SPIRAL. The sticky portion of a web.

WEB. The silken fabric spun by a spider.

# BIBLIOGRAPHY

Bristowe, William S. *The Comity of Spiders,* Vols. 1 and 2. London: The Ray Society, 1939 and 1941.

Comstock, John H. *The Spider Book.* New York: Doubleday & Co., 1912; revised ed. Ithaca: Cornell University Press, 1940.

Emerton, James H. *The Common Spiders of the United States.* New York: Dover Publications, 1961.

Fabre, Jean H. *The Life of the Spider.* New York: Dodd, Mead & Co., 1913.

Gertsch, Willis J. *American Spiders.* Princeton, N.J.: D. Van Nostrand Company, 1949.

Kaston, Benjamin J. *How To Know The Spiders.* Dubuque, Iowa: Wm. C. Brown Company, 1953.

McCook, Henry C. *American Spiders and Their Spinning Work.* Vols. 1–3. Philadelphia: published by the author, 1889–1894.

Savory, Theodore H. *The Biology of Spiders.* London: Sidgwick & Jackson, 1928.

———. *The Arachnida.* London: Edward Arnold & Co., 1935.

Warburton, Cecil. *Spiders.* Cambridge: The University Press, 1912.

# INDEX